NEW TACTICAL
GAMES
WITH DICE AND CARDS

Reiner Knizia

NEW TACTICAL
GAMES
WITH DICE AND CARDS

Reiner Knizia

BLUE TERRIER PRESS

NEW TACTICAL GAMES WITH DICE AND CARDS

Credits

Elfer Raus photograph on page 143 by Heiko Tobien [https://de.wikipedia.org/wiki/Elfer_raus!#/media/File:ELFER_RAUS!.jpg] and used in accordance with Creative Comons Attribution-ShareAlike 4.0 International License [https://creativecommons.org/licenses/by-sa/4.0/deed.en].

Dedicated to Inspector Cotta

3 4 5 6 7 8 9

CONTENTS

◆ New Tactical Games with Dice and Cards

FOREWORD
TO THE
ENGLISH EDITION

When I originally started to write this book, I was an unpublished author. I had a few games represented in magazines, but not a single boxed game on the market. Today, the archive of my works contains more than 600 published games in more than 2000 boxed editions, and more than 20 million copies have been sold all over the world.

What a difference half a lifetime makes when you dedicate yourself to fulfilling your dream!

Over the course of those years, a number of games in this book developed into fully fledged boxed games with specifically adapted materials.

It's interesting to see how some of the games evolved. Goldrush was published as a Wild West card game under its original title *Goldrausch*, Goal became a soccer card game *Tor*, Swap was developed into the recently published board game *Polynesia*, Sono became the tile laying game *Robot Master*, and Card Chase is now the card game *Escalation*.

But, what makes this book unique, is that you can play all the games presented here with standard playing materials like cards, dice and a few counters.

The text of this English edition remains faithful to the original German edition. It is packed with lots of timeless games, all exciting and stimulating. Therefore, I will stop here and let the games speak for themselves.

So many games to play, so little time! Enjoy!

Reiner Knizia

PREFACE

In a good game, even the losers win. It is the process of playing which is important, and the chance to interact and compete with other people. The appeal of the game is the time we spend together.

While we are playing, it feels like we are visiting new worlds and being subjected to different rules that measure our strengths. Each time, new skills and strategies are required. Everyday life is soon forgotten, previously unknown goals and exciting challenges are calling us. While playing, we become free to do things and take on roles that everyday life cannot offer us. We put aside our fears and embrace a new identity.

For this, we neither need endless rules nor lavish setups and equipment. It is what you do during the game and the choices that you make that provide the excitement. The rules set the boundaries, but within them we control our own world. We know our options and fight for success against our competitors.

Playing games, more than anything else, is make-believe. It is we, the players, who put life into the game and find elements in the form of new strategies. But we have to start with a situation that is defined by good and interesting rules. Then everyone wins, no matter who is victorious at the end.

In this book, I want to introduce you to a variety of new games. All of these can be played without special equipment or having to study long rulebooks.

All that you need is two standard playing card decks (each with 52 cards plus the jokers), some dice, some chips, and something to write with.

In addition to giving you the rules, I have tried to offer basic hints regarding game tactics. I have also tried to provide a number of suggestions for variants or even new game creations based on particular general concepts. What that means is that this book can also be seen as a collection of ideas for new games.

Now it's time to join the game and join the fun!

CARD GAMES
FROM ACE THROUGH KING

The oldest evidence of playing cards comes from China and dates back about 1200 years. In Europe, card games have been around for more than 600 years and, because gaming and gambling were frowned upon in more puritanical times, in many places it was known as "the devil's prayer book". Initially painted on leather, wood, silk or even hammered metal, playing cards soon benefitted from the manufacturing of paper and printing technology.

The sheer variety in card games is second to none. The line-up ranges from simple games of luck to complex masterpieces which require lots of concentration and experience. Every single deck of cards offers a nearly endless stream of exciting games. If we also use special cards in addition to the standard deck, we can create the most flexible set of gaming components in existence.

Typically, a shuffled deck of cards provides a new configuration every time we start a new game and offers a good mix of tactics and luck. By contrast, in this chapter you will find a group of quick games in which players will receive the same initial set of cards and where turns are played simultaneously.

Goal

Number of Players : 2 or more
Length : 15 minutes
Components : Game board, 52 cards, 1 chip

Game Concept:

It's all about goals. Whoever scores more goals than their opponent wins the game. The game takes place over two halves. Both players randomly choose a card from their hand. The higher card decides in which direction the ball will move. This way, the ball moves back and forth until...GOAL!

Requirements:

Copy the soccer field pictured below or you can easily draw it yourself. The playing area consists of two halves with three spaces each: the large midfield, the penalty box, and the small goal area. You will also need a small game chip (or coin) to represent the ball and a standard deck of 52 cards.

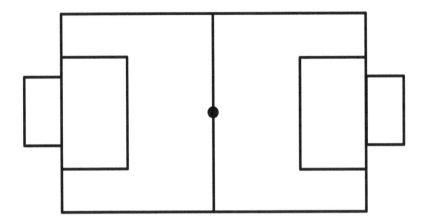

Setup:

The game has a duration of two halves. At the beginning of each half, both players receive thirteen cards of the same suit, from Ace through King, one receiving Hearts and the other Spades. Agree on which player owns which goal and put the ball (the chip or coin) in the middle of the playing area for the kick-off.

The thirteen cards correspond to the eleven team members and two substitutes, which you can use in each half. Each player has different strengths. A higher spot card (Two to Ten) beats a smaller one, face cards (Jack to King) are higher than all spot cards, with Jack being the lowest and King being the highest face card. An Ace beats all face cards, but is considered lower than the spot cards.

Gameplay:

Each half consists of thirteen rounds. During each round, you and your opponent choose a card and reveal them simultaneously. Whoever has the higher card wins the duel and moves the ball one space in the direction of the opponent's goal. If it's a tie, the ball doesn't move.

From the kick-off spot in the middle, the ball will initially move into one of the two big midfields. After that, it will move from space to space, ignoring the kick-off spot.

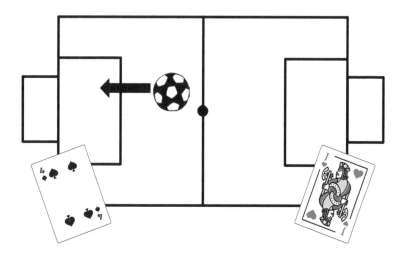

If you manage to move the ball into your opponent's goal, you score a goal. Afterwards, the game resumes from the kick-off spot.

It is important that each card is only used once per half and then has to be discarded face-down. After all thirteen cards have been played, that half is over.

Game end and overtime:

Usually, the game is over after both halves. Whoever has scored the most goals wins the game.

If there is a draw after both halves, you will begin a "sudden death overtime". Play until the first person scores another goal, which then wins the game.

Game tactics:

The Ace has exceptional position compared to the other cards. As long as you have your Ace, your opponent will be plagued with uncertainty – especially in critical situations in front of the goal: you could use the Ace against his face cards. If he tries to beat your Ace with a spot card, you could surprise him with a higher spot or a face card. If he considers this and wants to keep the upper hand by playing a face card, he will have to fear your Ace again.

Once your Ace is gone, your opponent will be able to put pressure on you with his face cards. Therefore, be careful with your Ace! But not too much so, because your opponent will adapt to your behavior.

In order to win a particular round, it's not important how much higher your card is than your opponent's card. To beat a 4 with a King is a costly victory, as your opponent will save important resources for later. To lose with your own 9 against a 10 is painful, as with roughly equal stakes your opponent will gain the advantage. Therefore, it is sometimes advisable to let your opponent waste a high card by playing a low card even in precarious situations. But maybe not too low, as your opponent might think the same way. You might even keep the upper hand with a relatively worthless card.

The game also has a mental component. Study your opponent! Try to memorize which important cards your opponent has already played and which options he has left.

It is usually advisable to attack your opponent in his own side of the field rather than having to defend your own goal. You may wish to pressure your opponent from the beginning and not allow him to get started properly. But make sure not to exhaust your options too early.

Championships and cups: As a short two-player game, it is also possible to arrange championships and cups with any number of players.

In a championship, each player will play against every other player. You may also decide to not use overtime or to only play one half per game. The winner of a match will be awarded two points, and in case of a draw, the points will be shared. Whoever has the most points at the end wins the championship. Should players have an equal amount of points, the larger margin (number of total goals scored minus goals scored against them) decides the winner.

With cups, a knockout system is used. To start, we will have to randomly determine the matchups for the first round. (You should pad the number of players with byes to 4, 8, 16 or 32 etc. and make sure that no two byes are matched against each other. Whoever is matched with a bye automatically advances to the second round.) Whoever loses is out of the cup. For the remaining participants, new matchups will be drawn. At the end, only two players will remain who will fight for the decisive victory.

Suggestions:

If you like, you can also use additional special cards besides the Ace. For example, you can designate a card as a central defender who causes the ball not to be moved in that round, thus eliminating one of your opponent's higher cards. Or as a long-range shot which moves the ball two spaces when the opponent plays a spot card.

Additionally, you can assign special abilities to certain cards when they occupy particular spaces (striker, central players, defenders, goal keeper) until the game consists of nothing but special cards. In that case, you might want leave the standard deck behind and create your own cards with funny and colorful figures. You play with your eyes!

Tennis Variant

Are you more interested in Tennis rather than Soccer? No problem! You can also use the following game board with only four spaces. (The horizontal lines are only for visual appearance and have no effect in the game.)

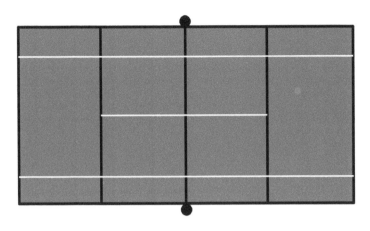

Gameplay

Just like in real tennis, the ball does not start on the court. In this variation, you are the server. You can flip a coin to see who serves first.

Again, during each round, you and your opponent choose a card and reveal them simultaneously. If you lose the first serve due to your opponent playing a higher card (like a "fault" in actual tennis), you still have a second chance. A subsequent loss would be a "double fault" and mean losing a point to your opponent. If the serve is successful, the ball flies into your opponent's space behind the net.

If your opponent is not able to return the ball in the next round, the ball will move another space closer to the opponent's baseline. Now your opponent is in a precarious situation, because if he loses again, the point is yours.

After each successful return (no matter from which position), the ball will fly into the space behind the net on the side of the player who lost the round. This way, the game goes back and forth. If the ball is not repelled in the following two rounds, the next point is made.

Whoever manages to score a point will serve during the next round. After every thirteen rounds, players receive new cards without resetting the game. To win the set, you need at least four points and must have at least two points more than your opponent. At the beginning of the game, you should agree on how many sets are played.

A wide variety of sports can be played with similar changes: hockey, volleyball, wrestling, rugby, boxing and more. Try it yourself!

Tower of Babel

Number of Players : 2 or 3
Length : 10 minutes
Components : 52 cards, 3 Jokers, 1 die

Game Concept:

Build the highest tower by accumulating the most points. Round after round, all players will simultaneously reveal one of their cards. The player with the highest card receives additional points depending upon how many rounds he has already won consecutively. Whoever has the most points at the end wins the game.

Requirements:

For this simple game, we need a standard deck of 52 cards, two Jokers (or three if there are three players) and a die (as big as possible so it's easy to move and see).

Setup:

Give each player the thirteen cards from Ace through King (a different suit for each player, plus a Joker). Place the die in the middle of the playing area.

The usual rank order of the cards (Two to Ace) applies. The Jokers are special cards.

Gameplay:

A game takes place over fourteen rounds. During each round, all players simultaneously reveal one of their hand cards.

The player with the highest card wins the current round and will now be the Builder of the Tower of Babel. For this, the "Builder" takes the die and puts it in front of himself, showing the number one. Only when have the die will you be able score points in the following rounds.

If a round is won by the player who already is the Builder, they receive as many points as the die shows. With each successive win, they increase the number the die shows by one.

If a round ends in a draw due to multiple players having played the same highest card, the current Builder of the Tower of Babel keeps the die, receives the corresponding points and can increase the number of the die again. If the die has not yet been claimed by a player, in case of a tie it remains in the center of the playing area.

The Builder will only lose their title when another player manages to win a round and becomes the new Builder. Turn the dice over to show the number one again.

The Builder will also lose their title when exactly one Joker is played during a round. In this case, the die will be put back into the center of the playing area. If multiple Jokers are played during a round, it is considered a tie and the Builder can score as usual.

Game end:

If a player manages to win a round when the die shows a six, they instantly win the game. This tends to only happen in rare cases.

Usually, you will play until all fourteen rounds are over. Then, the player with the most points wins. If two players have the same number of points, the one who was the Builder last wins the game.

Game tactics:

It's not important to be the Builder as often as possible; it's much more important to hold the title as long as possible. This increases the points you receive with each round. Similarly, you have to prevent your opponents from doing the same. Use your Joker, if necessary.

The longer a player holds the title of Builder, the more vicious the struggle becomes. Don't react too late and try not to cause any ties in a three-player game, which only benefits the current Builder. (Making agreements with other players is, of course, not allowed!)

The situation becomes especially interesting when the Builder plays their own Joker to neutralize a possible Joker from an opponent. It is a risky gamble that can pay off during certain situations, but also can have dire consequences.

Suggestions:

Instead of increasing the score by one point per round, you can double it to make the game even more fast-paced.

As a variation, you can shift the focus from the highest to the lowest card in a three-player game. The player with the lowest card then becomes the underdog and loses more points the longer they have this position. Here it is all about bluffing your way through and making it more difficult for other players. The Joker now has a different effect, as it will free you from being the underdog.

Or try an even simpler variant: the player who manages to win three consecutive rounds (or even any four rounds) wins. Try to keep your calm, as now the battle will start anew from the beginning.

Mr. President

Number of Players: 2 or 3
Length: 20 minutes
Components: Game board, 52 cards

Game Concept:

The goal is to secure enough votes to be elected president! During each round, the players compete for a different voting district. All players simultaneously select a card, and the player with the highest card wins. Whoever has the highest score in a region will receive the votes from that region. At the end of the game, the player with the highest amount of votes becomes president.

Requirements:

A complete deck of 52 cards and the map below. The precise shape of each district is not important, however, you should make a version that is big enough so each space can hold a card.

The thirteen spaces of the map represent voting districts and carry the symbols ranging from Two of Clubs to Ace of Clubs.

The individual voting districts form six different regions. As you can see, there are three regions with one district, two regions with three districts and one region with four districts.

Each region has been assigned a certain "voter value", as indicated by the numbers in the solid colored circles. Depending on size, each region has two to seven voters.

As an example, the region in the lower right of the map is composed of three districts (represented by the 5, 6, and 7 of Clubs). Winning the region is worth 5 votes, as indicated by the 5 on the solid circle.

Setup:

Separate the cards into suits. Shuffle the thirteen cards from Ace through King of Clubs and place them into a face-down stack. Give each player a different one of the remaining suit stacks.

Play with the regular order of cards: the Two is the lowest, Jack comes directly after 10 and the highest card is the Ace.

Gameplay:

The game takes place over thirteen rounds. At the beginning of each round, reveal the top card of the stack of Clubs cards to determine the contested district for this round.

Then, each player chooses a card from their hand and reveals them simultaneously. The player with the highest card wins and places his card face-up on the contested district on the map. The cards played by the other players are put aside face-down. In case of a tie, the district stays neutral and a face-down card is placed on it.

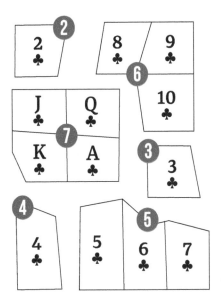

Game end:

After thirteen rounds, when all districts have been assigned, the game ends. Then, the votes of the six regions will be distributed amongst the players:

If you have more cards in a region than your opponents, you receive all the votes from that region.

In a tie, the decision is made based on the highest card. For example, in the biggest region (7) composed of four districts, if two players each have two districts and their highest cards are the same, the decision will be made based on their other two cards. If a decision still cannot be made, the voters of the affected region will stay neutral.

Whoever has the most votes at the end wins the game. If two players have the same number of votes, the player who won more regions is the winner. If the players have the same number of regions, then the player with the most districts wins.

For example, the end game situation pictured below result in five votes for Spades (Region 5) and ten votes for both Hearts (Regions 6 and 4) and Diamonds (Regions 7 and 3). Region 2 is neutral. Since Hearts and Diamonds have the same number of regions (2 each), they are still tied. A count of the individual districts reveals that Hearts has won three districts and Diamonds has won four. Diamonds will become Mr. President!

Game tactics:

Clear goals are required! Prioritize your actions and adapt your behavior to the situation at hand. Be wary of being bogged down. Trying to win every battle may result in losing everything.

There are 27 votes to be gained, if some regions don't tie and stay neutral. In a two-player game, you only need 14 votes for a sure victory. The two biggest regions alone aren't quite enough for that. A more comprehensive strategy will be required. In a three-player game, eleven points are sufficient for the presidency. The three single districts are not enough for that, so some commitment will also be required in the bigger regions.

Don't underestimate the smaller regions. You could possibly gain up to four votes in a single round. That could even be worth your Ace. Take care that your high cards don't end up in ties, or your Ace would be used for no gain. When you play multiple games, you should also try to analyze the behavior of your opponent and use it to your advantage.

In the big districts, it is to your advantage to be able to place one of your high cards at the very beginning. This will discourage your opponents in the following rounds. Pay attention to cards already placed in a region when a district is available there. Is it still possible to gain the majority? Which high cards do your opponents still have at their disposal? How many more votes do you still need in order to win? Who is your biggest adversary?

Variant: Vox Populi

If the regular game is too calm for you (which is atypical for politics!), the three-player game can be modified. If you have a second deck of cards, the game is even more exciting with four players.

The decision in the individual districts will not be made with the single highest card anymore. Now, you can only win by having the majority of all revealed points. For this, you will first have to determine the sum of the cards. The spot cards keep their stated value, Jacks are worth 12, Queens 13 and Kings are worth 14 points, whereas the Ace is worth 20 points.

If you cannot reach the required absolute majority with your cards alone, you will need the support of the other players. Persuasions and promises for the coming rounds will be necessary to make people use their points for you instead. As usual, you will put your card on the districts you win. The other cards from this round are put aside face-down. If no agreement can be made, the district stays neutral.

As you are not able to do much by yourself, you have to negotiate and cooperate in order to win. That means you have to help your opponents to further your own agenda. This probably won't be an easy task, as the closer you get to victory, the more the other players will unite against you. Don't exhaust your resources too early and keep some strong cards for the end—you will have to make the final push to victory on your own.

When all districts have been played, the scoring is the same as in the regular game. Alternatively, you can also award the individual regions to the player who has more points there than any other player. The fight for points has begun. Again, ties are broken with the highest card.

Suggestions

The broad field of politics also gives us many opportunities for variants of the game's principles. You can start by changing the distribution of the districts within the individual regions. By connecting the district Five of Clubs with Four of Clubs, which barely requires any modification of the game board, you have already created a new situation.

Or give every player a Joker. Here's how that would work. In the normal game, all players simultaneously reveal their card as they compete for each district. If a player uses his Joker, after the cards are revealed, he has the option to replace it with any card from his hand. As with the other cards, the Joker can only be used once and will be put aside face-down afterwards.

You can also use the Joker with a different ability, if you allow players to be able to play one or two cards at once. When playing two cards the sum of both cards counts for you. The Joker now is without value or importance. It can be used as many times as you wish and will be put back into your hand after each round. Its only purpose is for bluffing, which means you can concentrate your power even better and ignore other districts completely by playing only the Joker and nothing else.

Aside from politics, there are many other suitable themes that can based on the general idea of this game. Players could be building tycoons, vying for connected properties to create the most valuable building project. Or dare to be the first to cross the "Swamps of Somorrha" and be the first to establish a connected pathway through the following territory:

GOLD RUSH

In the 19th century, the discovery of gold in Alaska, Australia, South Africa and the United States sparked an unprecedented "gold-fever". Gold was first found in Sacramento Valley in 1848 and many thousands rushed to California to make their fortune. Because of this, gold seekers and settlers were lured into the remotest corners in the west of the USA. In many places the dream of easy wealth vanished as quickly as it had appeared. Often only ghost towns were left behind.

Only a few prospectors reached their goal of riches and prosperity. Most of the gold seekers had to content themselves with a very modest yield or went away empty-handed.

If you were there at that time you would have to ask "Where are the most promising mining sites?" and "Where should I set up my claim?". You would not only worry about finding the gold, but also how to defend your claim against poachers maneuvering to get a portion of your hard-won fortune. Now it's time to enter the world of gold miners and try your luck....

Gold Rush

Number of Players: 2 to 5

Length: 15 minutes

Components: Two decks of 52 cards plus two jokers

Game Concept:

Players take turns drawing a card. Gold or rock cards are played into one of the six claims immediately, whereas claim cards can be kept or put back. Each player can only take a maximum of three claim cards throughout the course of the whole game. When all cards have been played, the value of each claim is determined and divided between the claim cards. The player with the highest score wins.

Requirements:

We need two decks of 52 cards and two Jokers in order to create a special deck consisting of 66 cards. You can see the exact contents of this deck, including the card values and designations in the table below:

Cards	Quantity	Designation
red Ace (value 1)	4	18 **gold** cards (total value 60)
red Jack (value 2)	4	
red Queen (value 3)	4	
red King (value 4)	4	
Joker (value 10)	2	
black Two to black Seven	4 each	6 **claim** numbers 18 **rock** cards
red Two to red Seven	4 each	24 **claim** cards

This deck can be used for three to five players. With two players, some cards should be removed. You can find the details for this at the end of the rules section of the regular game.

Setup:

Create the card deck as described above. Put one set of a black Two to Seven, in a column, in the middle of the playing area. This will represent the six different claims (with the claim numbers "2" to "7"). On the right of each of these claim numbers, a growing number of gold and rock cards will be placed during the course of the game. The area to the left of the claim numbers will be used for claim cards that are put back.

Claims

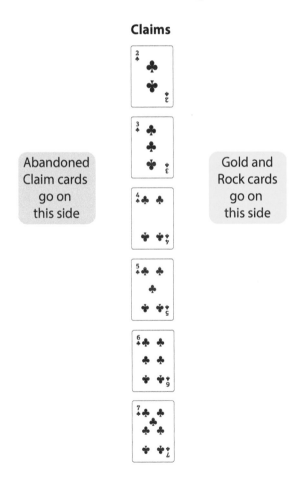

Abandoned Claim cards go on this side

Gold and Rock cards go on this side

Shuffle the remaining 60 cards to form a face-down deck. Agree on who will be the first player.

Gameplay:

Players take turns one after the other. During your turn, reveal the top card of the deck. You then have different options, depending on the kind of card you drew:

A gold or rock card has to be placed immediately next to a claim of your choice (to the right of the claim number). The gold cards (these are the red face cards and the Jokers) will be placed face-up, whereas the worthless rock cards (these are the remaining black cards valued 2 through 7) will be placed face-down.

Each claim can gather a maximum of six gold or rock cards during the course of the game, after which it is depleted. Additional gold or rock cards cannot be placed next to such a claim any longer, but have to be placed next to other, undepleted, claims.

However, if you reveal a claim card (i.e. a red suit card with a value of 2 through 7) you can choose between keeping the card by putting it face up in front of you, thus "staking a claim" and sharing in future profits. Or, you can abandon the claim by placing the claim card next to the claim number.

During the whole game **you can only take a maximum of three claim cards**, which are placed face-up in front of you. Once you place them, you can't put back, exchange or trade these cards.

The playing area will fill up with more and more cards during the course of the game. The value of the various claims will become clearer and clearer and it will become more obvious who owns what. You can find an example of a developing game situation on the next page:

Claims

Game end:

When the whole deck is used up, the game is over. Each claim then has been filled with six gold or rock cards, and all players each have chosen up to three claim cards.

Game scoring:

Now it's time to determine the value of each claim! I go into some detail here, but once you've played a couple of times, it goes very quickly.

For each claim, add together all the point values of the gold cards to its right. Once again, the values are:

Card	Point Value
Ace	1
Jack	2
Queen	3
King	4
Joker	10

The players with owned claims have a right to share in that claim. To find out how many players have owned claims we take the maximum possible of four and subtract the number of abandoned claims card to the left. Then divide this claim's gold total by the number of owned claims on it. Round the result down to the next whole number, if necessary, and add the resulting number of each claim to the score of each player with an active claim.

For example, let's take a look at the first claim—"2"—in the finished game situation **as pictured on the pages 38 and 39**:

The "2" claim has a total value of 17. That is computed as follows:

The gold and rock cards are to the right of the claim. They are valued as:

Queen = 3 / Face Down = 0 / Joker = 10 / Ace = 1 / Queen = 3 / Face Down = 0

So...

3 + 0 + 10 + 1 + 3 + 0 = 17 points

Claim "2" also has one abandoned claim card, so that means there are three "owned" claims. Each of the three owned claims is worth 5 points. That is computed as follows:

a) Divide this claim's gold total by the number of owned claims on it.
   17 / 3 = 5.67

b) Round the result down to the next whole number if necessary.
   5.67 rounds down to 5
   Therefore, each claim on "2" is worth 5 points.

Only one player has kept a claim card from claim number "3", which means the one owned claim gets the total value of 7 points. (The face down cards are worth zero. The King = 4 and the Queen = 3 for a total of 7 points.)

The value of claim number "4" is not important since all four claim cards have been abandoned; no player is entitled to receive any points from it.

Claim "5" is worth 4 points for each owned claim. That is computed as follows:

a) Joker = 10 / Jack = 2 / Ace = 1 / King = 4 / Face Down = 0 / Jack = 2
   so...
   10 + 2 + 1 + 4 + 0 + 2 = 19 points
   19 / 4 = 4.75

b) Round the result down to the next whole number if necessary.
   In this case, 4.75 rounds down to 4
   Therefore, each claim on "5" is worth 4 points.

The remaining claim cards with the numbers "6" and "7" are worth two and nine points to their owners, respectively.

Whoever has reached the highest total score wins the game.

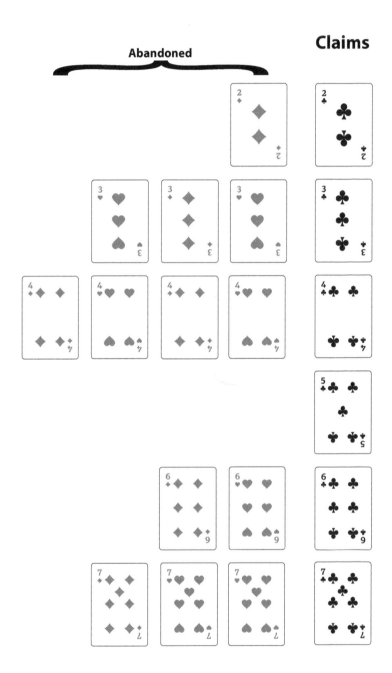

Gold & Rocks

If you want to play multiple games consecutively, you should add the scores of each player together across the games. At the end, the player with the highest total score wins.

Game tactics:

During the game, you can influence the composition of your own claim cards as well as the development of all claims. The choice of your own claim cards is the most important:

A claim card will bring you more points as more gold cards of high value are added, but the more other claims there are the smaller your share will be. Generally speaking, higher scoring claims will also have the most taken claim cards, which will reduce the score again. If you can limit sharing to a smaller number of players, you can often score more points with a lesser yielding claim.

Therefore, don't stake claims too early. Only as the game progresses will you be able to estimate the value of claims more accurately. If you have to choose your claims early, the other players may fill "your" claim with rocks very quickly, leading to a meager yield. However, should you manage to create a valuable claim your opponents will have enough time to share your success, which will decrease your share considerably.

On the other hand you also should not wait too long to choose your claim cards, because the longer the game goes on the higher the chance you will not be able to reveal enough claim cards and miss out, or end up having to choose a less than optimal claim card. Therefore you should keep track of the balance between claim cards that you have already taken and claim cards that are still available in the deck. Always consider the chance of a better card showing up.

With four players, for example, you can expect approximately six claim cards, so that you should on average keep every other card. The average value here is around five points per claim card and 15 points per player.

Aside from choosing the claim cards, the distribution of your revealed gold and rock cards in the individual claims is also important. Of course you will assign gold cards to "your" claims and rock cards to "opposing" claims. Especially towards the end, however, you should be aware which gold cards are still available in the game. You should pay attention to the two Jokers in particular, which are responsible for a third of the total gold yield in the game.

Gold Rush for two players

As mentioned before, you should use a smaller deck of just 48 cards in a two player game. The game becomes much faster and more interesting as a result. The following table will tell you the necessary details:

Cards	Quantity	Designation
red Ace (value 1) red Jack (value 2) red Queen (value 3) red King (value 4) Joker (value 10)	3 3 3 2 1	12 **gold** cards (total value 36)
black Two to black Seven	3 each	6 **claim** numbers 12 **rock** cards
red Two to red Seven	3 each	18 **claim** cards

Now, there are **only three claim cards of each claim** in the game and aside from that, **a claim is depleted after only four gold or rock cards**. The game is the same as before otherwise.

Make sure that you always have a claim card of an undepleted claim, or else you will not able to use gold cards for yourself that you reveal during the course of the game. The danger of "your" claim being filled with rock cards is not as present with only one opponent.

With two players you will be tempted to split the six claims, so that you will have three claims, and your opponent the other three. However, when making the decision of choosing the claim card of a neutral claim or rather that of an "opposing" claim, you should also account for the reduction of your opponent's points. If you can't count on being able to score at least as many points with the neutral claim as with the "opposing" one, you should join the claim of your opponent. This way, you can at least ensure a tie, whereas otherwise you might be able to score more points with your own claim, but still will fall behind compared to your opponent.

Variant: Long Gold Rush

Replace any four rock cards in the deck (for two or more players) with four black Aces. These four Aces are "stop" cards. When you reveal one of these cards, you have to immediately assign it face-up to a claim of your choice (just like a gold card). The corresponding claim then counts as depleted, and no more cards can be placed there.

In return, you are able to place as many gold and rock cards into a claim as you wish, as long as a stop card hasn't been placed there. The row to the right of the claim number can therefore become as big as the players choose.

The scoring is the same as in the regular game, except each rock card will now reduce the score of a claim by one. (The total score of a claim can never fall below zero, however.) The black Aces have no value.

Due to the negative rock cards, you will earn fewer points in total but then again, the differences in value amongst the various claims is now much larger. Because there are four stop cards, two of the claims will stay open until the end of the game, which means they have the potential to become very valuable. Use the black Aces to stop your opponents and divert the gold cards to your favored claims.

You also should no longer keep a claim card based on a guess, as a stop card could mean a quick end of all hopes. Now you have to wait longer to be able to judge a situation more accurately. The risk of having to go empty-handed thus steadily increases.

In this variant, and also in the regular game, players can agree on being able to put back a claim card, if they draw a better one, while still only being able to hold three at most during all times. This way, you get more options to adapt to the current game situation, and the risk of not having enough claim cards at the end is considerably less likely. Nevertheless, you need to carefully consider your choices since once a card has been put back, it can no longer be acquired.

Variant: Blind Gold Rush

At the beginning of the game, put the six cards with the claim numbers face-down into the playing area. The assignment of the numbers of the individual claims only happens during the course of the game in this variant, without the six claim numbers influencing them.

Start the game by playing as before. Gold and rocks are added to claims as normal. During the course of the game, if you reveal a claim card which you want to discard, but it is not present in the playing area yet, you can put this card over one of the (still free) claim numbers.

Therefore, if there are no abandoned claim cards of your card's number, the first abandoned claim card placed on top of a "blind claim" (a face down claim card) assigns that number to the previously blind claim. If there are already assigned or abandoned claim cards of the same number as yours, you place yours next to them as normal.

While doing this, it is not necessary that you use the first claim card you receive to assign it this way. You can "blindly" keep this card and wait for a later connection to a claim. However, if during the course of the game no claim card of a certain number is put back, that number is not assigned and the corresponding claim cards are worthless. So, claims that have been connected to a claim number only have three additional claim cards available for the players to get.

The following page offers an example of a possible game situation:

Claims

In this variant you are facing the dilemma of only being able to assign a number to a (valuable) claim only by using your own claim cards. Most assignments therefore happen at the beginning, when no player wants to keep claim cards, or when a player reveals a copy of an already kept "blind" card. At the beginning, you are somewhat in the dark, but when a majority of the claims have been assigned, the game is back to its roots.

This variant becomes especially interesting if you allow the same number to be connected to multiple claims. For example, you can have more than one claim "4" if identical claim cards are put on two or more blind claims. (When scoring the corresponding claim cards at the end of the game, the total score of all assigned claims will be distributed.) Inevitably, some other numbers will not be able to be assigned to a free claim at all and therefore won't have any value to anyone. (Put the worthless claim cards with these numbers aside when they are put back).

Variant: Gold Run

As a modification to the regular game, you can auction off the individual claim cards after revealing them and sell them to the highest bidder.

For this variant you only need about 100 gold nuggets (chips or coins), of which 60 are distributed equally among the players. The rest are put aside somewhere in the playing area until scoring.

Initially, the game is played as if it was the regular game. However, when you reveal a claim card and want to keep it for yourself, you have to name a number of gold nuggets you are willing to pay for it. One after the other, each player can outbid that price, until a highest bid is found that no other player wants to surpass. The claim card goes to the player with the highest bid, who pays the corresponding number of gold nuggets by putting them with the others in the playing area.

If you reveal a claim card and want to abandon it, no other player is allowed to buy it either. A player who already has three claim cards is also no longer allowed to bid in an auction. (Alternatively, you can agree that each player is able to keep any number of claim cards. However, this fundamentally changes the scoring of all claims.)

When the deck is depleted, each player receives the score of their claim cards in gold nuggets. The player with the most gold nuggets wins. If you play multiple games consecutively, your final score of the previous game becomes your new starting amount of gold nuggets. If a player has lost all of their gold nuggets, they are out of the game.

Besides the choice of your claim cards this game now becomes a question of finding a reasonable price. Don't let yourself be tempted to pay excessive prices, you may be able to buy the same claim cards much cheaper later on. Particularly towards the end of the game, it is often the case that only a few players are still able to make bids, enabling you to buy cards very cheaply.

If you want to go one step further, you can allow players to make any kind of deal and payments with each other. Here, you should try to influence the placement of the individual gold cards or, in combination with the previous variant, even steer the assignment of the numbers and claims to get a good position. Exchanging claim cards between players is still forbidden even in this variant, however.

Suggestions

In Gold Rush, it really pays off to create custom cards. This way, you free yourself from the limitations of the 52 card deck card face designs which can make the playing field much clearer and more easily understood.

You can forget about the claim numbers and instead use six different colors. You don't even have to differentiate between the claim numbers and claim cards anymore. With four or five players, you can even add another claim card per color and therefore increase your tactical opportunities considerably.

Illustrate the various values on the gold cards with the corresponding number of gold nuggets on the card, so you can easily count the total score of the claims simply by counting the gold nuggets on the cards. Design the rock cards in a similar manner, but without any gold nuggets, and now you can play them face-up into the claims as well.

If you want to, you can even thematically alter the game to take place in the world of modern high finance. The claims become companies, the claim cards shares or stock, and the gold and rock cards are now revenue, which is now distributed among the shareholders at the end of a fiscal year. The game itself is not changed by this in any way, but maybe this theme will give you some inspirations for new variants.

COMPLICA

The origin of board games lies in the early cultures of the Orient. The oldest depictions come from temples and burial chambers of the old Egyptians and date back more than 5000 years.

The mystery of the rules to these games has not been passed down to us and might be lost forever. However, it is most likely that initially, cultic and mystical notions were present.

Many of the old board games symbolize combat and war situations. Others are more akin to races. A third group of games was also widely known, in which pieces are continuously distributed among a number of individual bowls.

In this chapter, you will find a simple placement game that will become more and more complicated with each new round.

Complica

Number of Players: 2
Length: 10 minutes
Components: Game board, 2 x 16 gaming pieces

Game Concept:

One after the other, the players slide their pieces from the right into the various rows of the game board. Whoever manages to have four of their own pieces in a line first (either in a row or column), wins the game.

Requirements:

We need 16 white and 16 black checkers pieces and the game board you see below.

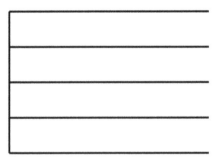

Ideally, the four rows of the game board should be limited in such a way that exactly eight pieces fit until a row is full. (As a start, a simple sketch on a piece of paper is sufficient, and depending on what you have at your fingertips, you can use chips or coins as playing pieces.)

Gameplay: Agree with your opponent on who plays with the white pieces, who plays with the black pieces, and who starts.

In alternating turns, you and your opponent slide one of your unused pieces into the first space in a row, possibly pushing pieces that are already there further into the row.

Which row you want to use is up to you. However, a row can only hold a maximum of eight pieces.

Also note the important additional rule: You cannot use the row your opponent used during their last turn unless no other row is free or the last three pieces on that row (on the positions 1 to 3) already belong to your opponent.

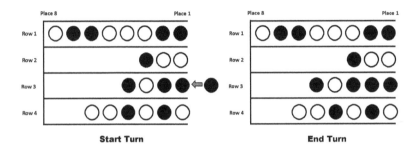

Game end:

If a player succeeds in having a line of four pieces of their own color in a row or one below the other in a column (no matter if due to their own or an opponent's turn), that player wins the game.

Illustration

If you and your opponent can manage to have the same amount of winning lines simultaneously, the game continues, until one player has a greater number of winning lines. If the game board is full and no one has a set of four in a row, the game ends in a draw.

For example, Black has to play into the first row in order to not lose the game immediately. The second row is already filled: pushing into the third row causes a black winning line, but also two white ones. By using the fourth row, only a white winning line is created.

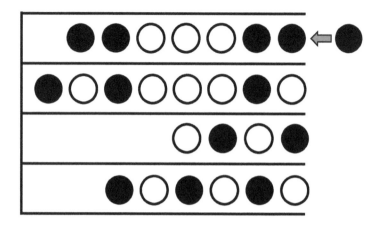

White wins during the next turn by playing into the fourth row:

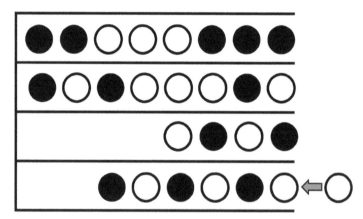

Game tactics:

Clearly, Complica becomes more complicated with each new piece. To be able to analyze the situation correctly, you should check if by using any of the four rows for your turn, you can win or at least get a significant advantage. Conversely, you should ask yourself what the most favorable move would be for your opponent in order to prevent this.

The forced moves that can be created by two pieces of the same color being in the positions 1 and 2 of the same row are of particular importance. As soon as you play a third piece of the same color, your opponent usually has to play into that row in order not to lose the game immediately. This way, you can move a particular row by two spaces without giving away your turn.

For example, White wins in the following situation by using the fourth row:

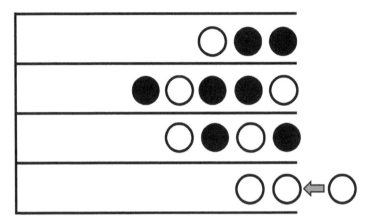

Black now MUST choose the fourth row, and White will have a winning line with the spaces in the fourth position by using the first row:

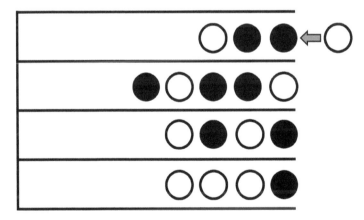

Successive pieces in the same row also have the advantage later in the game by not being able to be pushed out of a row as quickly. On the other hand, you will only be able to exert pressure on your opponent by distributing your pieces equally among all four rows.

Variant: Dia-Complica

You can increase the complexity of Complica by allowing four diagonal pieces in a line to count as a winning line.

This way, your options will be vastly increased, as the individual pieces will now be connected over a much greater number of potential winning lines. The possibilities of creating a situation in which your opponent will be forced to make a certain move are vastly increased.

Variant: Double-Complica

To increase the complexity even further, you can agree with your opponent on being able to play two pieces per turn. (In order to keep the game as symmetrical as possible, the first turn of the first player should be made with only one piece.) You can also choose the rows for your pieces completely independent from your opponent's previous turns here.

At the end of your turn, you usually shouldn't let your opponent have two consecutive pieces on the first two spaces in any row, as otherwise a winning row could be created there instantly. Consequently, there will be a fierce battle even around the first few spaces. The end of the game will also be reached much faster here than in the regular game. The deeper winning lines often will not happen at all. Therefore, you should try to keep your pieces relevant and push your opponent's into the deep end.

Suggestions

Complica is a game that could even be fun for computer experts: the board is easily recreated on the computer, the possible moves easily programmed and the winning lines have a very simple structure. As a result of previously played pieces, the potential winning lines will be more and more limited. As there are only four options when making your choice, the computer can calculate many turns ahead in a very short time and become very strong as a result. When have you ever been beaten by your own program?

Aside from the regular game with four rows for eight pieces each, you can of course also use bigger boards, for example with five or six rows. The length of the required winning lines can be kept at four pieces or adjusted to the number of rows.

At various times in this book I will pose some interesting questions for you to try to work out. Trying to answer these questions will not only help you to understand the game under discussion, but the way that games are constructed, and the underlying rules and possibilities associated with all games. Some of these questions may be difficult to answer, however I have provided you with a complete solution to each of the questions. These solutions can be found at the end of the book. Here is the first question for you to consider:

 Question 1

Three row Complica: If Complica is played with only three rows, there is a clear strategy for one of the two players to win the game every single time. What is this strategy? (The winning lines only consist of three pieces here. You are allowed to play into the row your opponent used during their last turn if the last two pieces in that row belong to your opponent.)

 Question 2

Trivial Complica: If we allow playing into the same row your opponent used during their last turn, there is a simple strategy to assure a tie. What is this strategy? Be aware that Complica should always end in a tie when both players play expertly.

We will come back to strategic considerations in the following section, "Excursion into Game Theory". But before that, a little more about "pushing":

Complica is a one-dimensional "pushing game", as the pieces can only be moved into one direction. However, it is not very hard to expand the game to use two dimensions:

Take a game board with 5 x 5 spaces and, in alternating turns, each player can push a piece onto any of the 16 border spaces. Already existing pieces will slide one space further in the direction of the push:

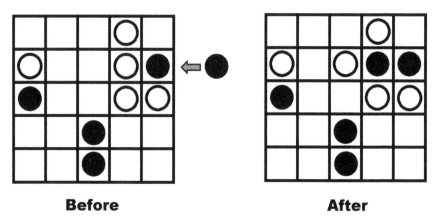

Before   **After**

However, you are only allowed to play a piece if all pieces will stay on the board. Consequently, no move can be made in a row already filled with five pieces.

Depending on which goal you set, you will decide the character of the game. In the style of Complica, you can strive for four consecutive pieces in a row (or even diagonally) in your own color. Or maybe you can try to surround your opponent's pieces. It is also possible to assign a value of three points to the center space and a value of one to the eight surrounding spaces, and the winner will be the player with the most points once the board has been filled.

You can also limit yourself to only be able to push horizontally, whereas your opponent will only use the vertical rows. Or use more pieces, and throw your opponent's pieces off the board. This is a vast field of possibilities.

EXCURSION INTO GAME THEORY

A few years ago, there was an interesting contest involving a game in which two players could either play cooperatively or selfishly.

If both players cooperated, they each received a reasonable prize. When both players chose to play selfishly, they both had a negative result. If two different strategies were chosen, however, the selfish player received a big prize, whereas the cooperative player received a great loss.

The interesting thing about this contest was that it wasn't people, but computer programs that played against each other.

Surprisingly, neither the naive programs which always cooperated nor the purely selfish systems were able to prevail. The clear winners were the programs which started cooperatively, and then used a "tit for tat" approach: punishing egoistical behavior of their opponent by also employing a selfish strategy, only to be ready to continue playing the game cooperatively if their opponent starts to cooperate.

This result could have been predicted by what mathematically oriented social scientists call "Games Theory". In that light, let us look at some fundamental considerations related to the theory of games and their strategies in the following chapter.

Excursion into Game Theory

Game theory is a mathematical system that concerns itself with the decision points (games), in which the conscious decision-makers (players) are in opposition to each other. Each decision-maker has many different options to act (strategies) at their disposal. When all decisions have been made, the consequences can be determined.

The real consequences are assigned to numerical values, so that the result for each decision-maker can be expressed with a single numeric value (which can be either positive or negative). It is based on the assumption that each decision-maker acts rationally and tries to maximize their gain.

Such decision situations not only occur in board games, but in nearly all social, economic or political conflicts. The mathematical game theory classifies games depending upon their nature and certain criteria, which we will use as guidelines for our short discussion:

Number of players: Of course, the number of active decision-makers in a game is of great importance. We distinguish between one player games, two player games, and multi-player games with more than two players.

The following "police problem" shows that one player games can still contain very interesting decision-making situations:

Five robbers meet in a building. Outside, a police officer waits, with the task of following the leader of the robbers. The police officer only knows that the leader is the physically tallest of the robbers. For safety reasons, the robbers leave the building separately, meaning the police officer can only follow the last one who just left the building.

Even though more than one person has an interest in how this game will end, this is only a one player game, since only the police officer is acting as a conscious decision-maker, whereas the robbers are not even aware of the game situation.

Question 3

Police problem: How would you act in the role of the police officer, if you can assume that the order, in which the individual robbers leave the building is completely random? How good are your chances – using an optimal strategy – of following the right robber? (Assume, that the police officer has no idea of the average height of the robbers.) How would you estimate your chances of success, if it was 100 robbers instead?

Questions of this sort will appear in situations where you have to immediately make a decision to take or ignore each option as they are presented to you one at a time.

Cooperation: Two men are accused of having committed armed burglary together and are imprisoned in separate cells. Both have the choice of making a confession or staying silent. If one confesses and the other one remains silent, the person who confessed will be freed in exchange for being a key witness, while the other one will be locked up in prison for 20 years. If both admit their guilt, they will each receive a sentence of five years. However, if both keep quiet, there won't be sufficient proof and both will only be sentenced to one year in prison for illicit possession of a firearm. The decision-making situation is summarized again in the following chart where the numbers represent the cost in terms of years spent in prison:

	Player 2 Confesses	Player 2 Stays Silent
Player 1 Confesses	Player 1: - 5 Player 2: - 5	Player 1: 0 Player 2: - 20
Player 1 Stays Silent	Player 1: - 20 Player 2: 0	Player 1: - 1 Player 2: - 1

How would you make your decision in this situation? If the other confesses, it would be better for you to confess as well and to be sentenced to jail for five years, instead of having to endure 20 years by remaining silent. However, if the other doesn't say anything, it would be a good idea to confess and go free instead of being convicted of possessing an illegal firearm. At any rate, you will be in a better position by confessing.

We can assume that the second prisoner will make the same considerations and therefore also confess, so that you both will go behind bars for five years. The paradox in this two player game (which is known as the "prisoner's dilemma") is that even with optimal strategies, you would have fared much better if both individuals keep quiet.

This same thing holds for two countries which want to achieve military superiority with appropriately high armament budgets, but end up equally strong and equally poor.

Obviously, it is of great importance which options of cooperation and communication are available. If negotiation is possible, it is usually best for each player if everyone plays cooperatively. Oftentimes, however, an unattractive, but collectively better option can be made more palatable for an individual player with side payments. In a multi-person game there is also the possibility of coalitions forming, which often break down when the players begin the final game of how to share the profits among the coalition partners.

There will be diametrically opposed interests, whenever there is a *zero-sum* situation. This is a situation where the sum of payouts to all players diminishes the available resources to zero. Nothing is added, and nothing is lost. A profit can only be made at the expense of others. Especially in two player games this doesn't leave any room for cooperation. An example of this is chess. (We can imagine that the winner will receive a point, the other player loses a point, and in case of a draw no points will be awarded.)

Information: When all players are completely informed about the previous events in the game, and also about the current situation and the available possibilities, it is considered a game with open information. There are no simultaneous turns or random influences. No player has more information than the other. Apparently, there is some secret or unavailable information in the police problem. However, most widely known board games have no secret information — for example chess.

Finiteness: If a game consists of a limited number of turns and every player only has a limited number of options during each turn, it is considered a finite game. Each player then only has a fixed or limited number of possible strategies.

Both the police problem and the prisoner's dilemma are finite games. The same is true for chess. The following "silent duel" is *not* a finite game:

A chicken lays an egg each night between midnight and 1 AM, with any given moment within this time interval being an equally likely time for the egg to appear. There are two thieves, who are not able to see each other from their starting positions, and each wants to steal the egg. Each of the two thieves is only allowed to go into the hen house once for a short time and can take the egg if it is there. If both arrive at the same time, neither will receive the egg.

There are an infinite number of moments in which both thieves can decide to look for the egg. If one of them finds the coop empty, he doesn't know whether his opponent was already there – so the duel takes place in total silence.

Obviously, a thief shouldn't go into the hen house too early, as the risk of the egg not having been laid yet is very high. On the other hand, it's not very wise to only appear after 1 AM in order to reduce the risk that your opponent has already checked, perhaps just moments earlier. Apart from that, your approach will be determined by how you expect your opponent to act.

Silent duel: What would you do in the role of one of the thieves, if you can assume that for each moment, it is equally likely for the other thief to appear? What are your chances – using an optimal strategy – to get the egg and what is the probability of success for your opponent?

Other duels are more "vocal". For example, there is the standard situation of two men, pistols drawn, running towards each other and each only able to fire one (or two or three) shots, with the probability of a hit rising with decreasing distance. Here, the duelists of course know whenever their opponent has fired a shot and can adapt their behavior accordingly.

The main theorem of game theory: To conclude our excursion, let's take a look at one of the most important findings of game theory. The main theorem of game theory states: each finite two-player zero-sum game with no secret information has a clearly determinable value. One player has a strategy to reliably win that value – no matter what the opponent's strategy is. The other player has a strategy with which – again not dependent on the first player – no more than that value will be lost.

This statement is highly interesting, as it tells us that all of these games will always end the same way, given both players play with an optimal strategy: if your opponent picks their strategy, it doesn't make sense for you not to use yours, as you will only risk an even lower score in the end.

And why should your opponent not use their strategy if they know that with your corresponding counterplay, they will get their best possible outcome? Only when you and your opponent both don't use your strategies will the result not be predetermined.

The most well known examples for finite two player zero sum games with no secret information are Chess, Go, Reversi, Lasca, Kalah or Twixt. (For some games the finiteness has to be enforced through the addition of an inconsequential rule, so that the game ends in a draw after a million turns at the latest.)

For chess, the main theorem of game theory has the consequence that one of the following three cases has to be true:

1. White has a winning strategy, with which they can always win, no matter what Black does.
2. Black has such a winning strategy.
3. Neither White nor Black has such a winning strategy, but both players have a strategy with which they are able to enforce a draw, no matter the strategy of their opponent.

Has chess become uninteresting now, because of this? No way! And with that, the current limitations of the mathematical game theory become apparent. That is because, we don't know which of the three cases is actually true, and even if we did we still would have no idea what the appropriate strategies of the player would actually look like. Only by knowing this would chess become trivial. Therefore, we will still be able to enjoy exciting chess matches for many years to come.

DICE GAMES
FROM ONE TO SIX

The oldest dice known to us only have four sides and are in the shape of a pyramid made of four triangles. They were found during excavations in the Sumerian royal tombs of Ur and are more than 5000 years old.

This unusual shape was very well known even to the Romans, though not to us nowadays. They used sheep ankles, which connect the shin to the heel, as suitable playing pieces. "Alea iacta est (the die is cast)" has been attributed to Caesar as he crossed the Rubicon.

A special kind of dice games are category games. These are based on a list of different scoring options and every player tries to fit their roll into one of the remaining categories. When the whole list has been filled, the player with the best assignments wins.

Yahtzee, Kniffel, Hindenburg, and Kameruner are probably the most common representatives of the category games. In this chapter, you will find a selection of new variants with different difficulties:

Six Hundred

Number of Players: 1 to 4
Length: 15 minutes per player
Components: 6 dice, score sheet

Game Concept:

The game is based on a scoring table with four different scoring categories—Numbers, Ladders. Figures, and Patterns. Together, they offer 18 different scoring opportunities. One after the other, the players roll the dice and write down their result in one of the appropriate boxes. When all categories have been filled, the player with the most points wins. Including the bonuses it is possible to reach a maximum of 600 points.

Components:

We need six dice and the score sheet pictured below, which you should copy.

Setup:

Agree on which player goes first and in which order you want to play. Write the names of the players into the first row on the score sheet accordingly, so that each player has their own column. During the course of the game, the score sheet should be easily visible to all players.

Gameplay:

Six Hundred takes place over 18 rounds, during which you will take your turn in order to fill an empty box in your scoring columns.

When it is your turn, begin by rolling all six dice. You can "set aside" dice to keep certain values as you try to satisfy a particular scoring opportunity. You can take any remaining dice (as many dice as you wish—even all of them if none have been set aside) and re-roll them. After your second throw, you again have the option to set aside dice (or not) and take any number of remaining dice and re-roll them a third and last time. However, any dice which you set aside earlier cannot be re-rolled on a later turn.

Your turn will end after the third roll, if not before, and you will have to decide in which free box in your scoring column you want to record your result. The choice is yours. During each turn exactly one assignment must be made, and boxes which have been filled already cannot be used again.

If, by choice or out of necessity pick a box in which your roll doesn't fit, this box will be crossed out and will score 0 points.

Make copies of the following score sheet to play:

SEE NEXT PAGE

Six Hundred

Players →					
Numbers	Ones				
	Twos				
	Threes				
	Fours				
	Fives				
	Sixes				
Numbers total					
36 for 80					
Ladders	1st Ladder				
	2nd Ladder				
	3rd Ladder				
	4th Ladder				
Ladders total					
Figures	Quadruplets				
	Quintuplets				
	Even				
	Odd				
Figures total					
Patterns	Singles				
	Twins				
	Triplets				
	Sextuplets				
Patterns total					
36 For 17					
Grand total					

Numbers category scoring:

From the Ones to the Sixes there are six number values. In these boxes you record the sum of all dice which show the required number.

For example, with the roll pictured below, you could be scoring 2 points with the Ones, 12 points with the Fours or 6 Points with the Sixes:

Altogether, it is possible to achieve a maximum of 126 points by completing all six number boxes. If you reach at least 80 points, you receive an additional bonus of 36 points.

Ladder scoring:

In the Ladders category, the full sum of all dice in a roll is recorded. The order you use the boxes in is up to you. However, once a ladder box has been completed, you are only allowed to record your score if the smaller ladders that have been filled already have a smaller result, and all assigned greater ladders have a higher score, respectively.

In the example below you can only enter the numbers 25 or 26 for the second ladder. In order to fill the fourth ladder, you would need a result of 28 or more points:

Six Hundred

Ladders	1st Ladder	24			
	2nd Ladder				
	3rd Ladder	27			
	4th Ladder				
Ladders total					

At the end of the game, the entries from the 1st to the 4th ladder – disregarding boxes which have been crossed out – must increase from one to the next. With optimal allocation you can score up to 138 points in this category.

Figure scoring:

In order to score Quadruplets or Quintuplets, your roll must have at least four or at least five dice with the same number, respectively. You will then be credited with the sum of **all** six dice. For example, you would receive 32 points for the following Quintuplets (or Quadruplets):

The categories Even and Odd require your roll to consist of 6 even and odd numbers, respectively. - The prior example shows an even roll. - Once again you will record the sum of **all** dice.

The maximum achievable value for completing all four figure scoring boxes is 138 points. (How so? If you roll six sixes, that can be scored in the

Quadruplets, Quintuplets, or Even boxes. In each case, you would receive 36 points which is the sum of all dice. The highest roll possible for the Odd box is six fives for a total of 30 points. Thus, 36 + 36 + 36 +30 = 138.)

Pattern scoring:

For each of the four pattern scorings all six dice have to fulfill certain conditions. Successfully completing a pattern achieves the preset number of points listed for the box, regardless of the actual numbers you rolled.

The first pattern is Singles. It consists of six unique dice, meaning that each number from One to Six shows up exactly once (27 points):

For Twins (30 points), you will need three pairs (for example, 1-1, 2-2, and 6-6), though they don't necessarily have to be different numbers. In the example below, there are two pairs of twos and a pair of fives (2-2, 2-2, 5-5).

Similarly, you need two sets of three identical numbers for Triplets (33 points). In the example below, there is a triplet of ones and a triplet of sixes (1-1-1 and 6-6-6):

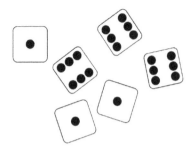

Lastly, a Sextuplet (36 points) consists of a roll with six of the same number.

In total, it is possible to score a maximum of 126 points by completing the four patterns.

Game end and overall scoring:

The game is over after 18 rounds when all boxes of the scoring rows have been filled.

Calculate the sum of all Numbers, Ladders, Figures, and Patterns. Don't forget to add the bonuses, if applicable.

If you were able to fill all boxes of your column – with the only possible exception of the Sextuplets – without crossing out any of the boxes, you will receive an additional bonus of 36 points.

It is possible (but very difficult!) to achieve a maximum of 600 points. Whoever has the highest total score at the end wins the game.

Game tactics:

Six hundred is not an easy dice game and not a game of chance in the slightest! Victory or defeat is mainly dependent on your tactical approach.

The possibility of re-rolling one or more dice a second or even third time can influence the result of your rolls considerably. Your decision of which box to fill during each turn is also of great importance.

If you fill up many of the easy categories at the beginning, you will slowly get into more and more trouble. If you try too hard to get the various bonuses, you will often find your points slipping through your fingers. If you take big risks to press your luck, the result may be underwhelming. If you play too carefully, you won't get far either. A happy medium and a consistent strategy are necessary.

After the first few rolls you will see that every game is different. In order to manage your odds effectively, you will need to keep track of all your unfilled scoring boxes and their required rolls.

During the course of the game, your options will continue to diminish. Therefore, it is important to manage your rolls effectively. Try to aim for the most complicated figure and pattern scorings early on, even if you have to take some risks to do so. In a nearly empty column, a failed roll can still fit in somewhere. Try to keep your balance to leave your options open.

The longer you can keep your ladders free, the more free space you have. It is not easy to have a considerable score in the lowest ladder and still be able to safely fill the higher ladders later on.

Make sure to not only meet the requirements of the figures, but to also get a score as high as possible. It pays to focus on the Fives and Sixes throughout the whole game, as they can be used profitably in many places. Five Ones and a Two may be Quintuplets, but they are still only worth seven points for you.

If during the course of the game you will get into the not so uncommon situation of having to cross out a box, you should start with the Sextuplets – not only is their appearance quite rare, but it will also allow you to keep the additional bonus of 36 points. If having to cross out additional boxes is unavoidable, you will have to decide yourself whether you want to cross out the not very profitable Ones and Twos of the number scorings (and lose the possible bonus that goes with it), or if you prefer a different solution. Be warned that the tempting bonus for the numbers will put you into a moral conflict from time to time.

Even as a one player game, six hundred retains its full potential, as multiple players don't affect each other anyway. You can still gather valuable experience without needing other players.

Variant: Thirty-six

Achieving the highest total score is not the only way to play. Alternatively, you (with a total of two to four players) can also score the results in the eighteen different categories on their own. The game is played like the regular game initially. As soon as all boxes of a category are filled or crossed out, however, this category will be scored immediately.If a player has managed to get a higher score in that category than every other player, that player will receive 2 points. If there is a clear second place, that player receives 1 point. If there is no single best player and the best result is shared by exactly two players, they will both still get 1 point. All other players and other situations are awarded no points. (At most, only two players may receive points for any given category.) A box which has been crossed out can't receive any points.

Make a record of these points in the corresponding boxes by making a visible dot behind the numerical result or in the total score row at the end of the score sheet. Once a particular scoring row is completed, you can use a diagonal line to mark the category. This makes scoring easier to keep track of:

Players ⟶		William	Jane	Andrew	
Numbers	Ones	3		5	
	Twos	10 ●	8 ●	4	
	Threes	9	12 ●	12 ●	
	Fours	16	20 ●	16	
	Fives	20	20	20	
	Sixes	24 ●	18	30 ●	
Numbers total					

After 18 turns and all boxes are completed (either with a score or crossed out), scoring ends. There are no bonuses.

Altogether, it is possible for the best player to reach a maximum of 36 points. Whoever has the highest total score wins the game.

The main difference of Thirty-six compared to the regular game is the tactics, as now there will be a considerable interdependency between the players. While previously it was important to have results as consistently high as possible, now only top scores count. As the patterns only have a fixed amount of points, it becomes about sharing a positive result with the least number of players as possible.

During the skirmishes with your opponents you will have to take higher risks. Take care not to cross out too many boxes. Where your opponent already has a top score, don't worry about putting a bad roll there. If you are the first to write down a result in a given category, try to do so with as high of a score as possible to not make it too easy for your opponents.

Especially in a two-player game, it is of great tactical importance which categories will be filled by you first and where your opponent chooses to become active. It is of course advantageous to let your opponent play first and wait for a higher roll to win that category—but your opponent will try to do the same. Since you can usually be second place in any category, you should try to avoid having to cross out any boxes, as you won't even get a single point that way.

Variant: Seventeen

An additional variant (for two to four players) is created by doing away with individual columns for each player. Don't fill the score sheet with the player names at the beginning, but give each player a pen in a different color instead.

Play the game as usual then, with the difference that each player records their result with their pen in the first column of the corresponding category.

If during the course of the game a category has a result already (entered by you or your opponent), you can only choose that category if your result is higher than the current entry. In this case, cross out the prior score and write yours into the next column. Additional entries in the same category can happen the same way.

Figures	Quadruplets	~~18~~	24		
	Quintuplets				
	Even	28			
	Odd	~~16~~	~~22~~	26	
Figures total					

Instead of using differently colored pens, you can also mark entries with your initials.

In contrast to the regular game, the Singles box is removed from the game entirely, so that only 17 scoring categories remain. For the other scoring patterns, we will also use the sum of all six dice instead of the preset value. This way, we will be able to improve on scores in these categories as well over the course of the game.

With the ladders, you will only be able to record your score in a lower ladder when all higher ladders have at least one entry with a higher score than your current roll.

Each turn has to be recorded on the scoring sheet and if you have no other options, you might have to record a score of 0 in a previously unassigned category. As soon as the seventeenth and last category receives an entry, the game ends.

Only the highest score in each category counts and is awarded 1 point. Crossed out results are disregarded. Whoever has the most points at the end wins the game.

Tactics-wise, each turn offers you three options: you can surpass an opponent's result, fill an empty category, or improve your own score. Usually, you should plan your turns by this order. In the first case, you will take away a point from your opponent, in the second you will at least receive a point, whereas the third option will not immediately increase your total score.

With more than two players, you should of course try to surpass the scores of your most dangerous opponent. However, don't let yourself be blinded by a good standing in the middle of the game. Only the best scores will last until the very end. Don't think short-term, as whoever owns many categories also has many possible weak points.

Only when the end is already in sight and only few categories are left can you hope to keep a category with a low score. Force the end of the game by taking over unassigned categories when you are in the lead.

Suggestions

It is obvious that Six Hundred offers a vast field of possible variants:

As a start, you can change the number and type of categories in any way you wish and play with more or fewer dice. Feel free to do away with re-rolling or even allow scoring in multiple categories at once.

Of course, you also have the option to change how the game ends. Having to fill all categories as quickly as possible or having to reach a certain amount of points can also provide some fun and interesting variations.

Catego

Number of Players: 2 to 4
Length: 5 minutes per player
Components: 2 dice, score sheet

Game Concept: Players take turns rolling the dice and record their result in one of the free columns in their row. Whoever has the highest result in a column will receive points equal to the value of that column. Whoever earns the most points this way wins the game.

Components: For this simple category game we merely need two dice and a sketch of the following score sheet:

	2	3	4	5	6	7	8	9	10	11	12

The score sheet consists of eleven columns with the point values from two to twelve. Each player has their own row.

Setup:

Determine the first player and in which order you want to play. Enter the names of the individual players on the score sheet so that each player has their own scoring row.

Gameplay:

The game takes place over eleven rounds, with the players taking their turns in sequence. During your turn, you roll both dice and then decide which empty column in your row you want to assign your score to.

In the end, only the highest result in a given column counts. During the course of the game you should cross out lower results in a column and only leave the highest roll in any given column. In case of a tie, all results will be crossed out.

As soon as a column has been filled by all players, you can write the name of the winner into the box above its point value. This way, you will always have a clear overview:

	2	3	A 4	5	6	7	8	J 9	10	11	12
Steve			~~7~~	~~8~~				~~3~~	~~9~~		12
Jane			~~5~~	~~8~~	8			9			~~4~~
Alan	4		8		~~7~~			~~8~~	10		

Game end:

Catego is over after eleven rounds, after all columns of the score sheet have been filled completely. Each column already should have found its winner by then or should have been crossed out completely due to equal results. The number of points for a column is equal to the column label. In the above example, Alan rolled the highest score—an 8—in the column marked "4". So, as the winner of that column he is awarded 4 points.

Tally the points earned by each player. Whoever has reached the highest sum of points wins the game.

Game tactics:

It is possible to earn a maximum of 77 points (i.e., 2+3+4+5+6+7+8+9+10+11+12=77). Of course, the columns with the highest number of points deserve your attention. There are many good reasons to enter your best results there. If all of your opponents behave in the same manner, however, you won't be sure about who will win which columns. Therefore, it can also be wise to record your high rolls in somewhat lower value columns in order to ensure that you will be accumulating points.

Also keep track of the results of your opponents and try to place your high rolls wherever you have a high chance of winning the column. You can safely register your weak results in columns where another player already has placed a high result.

Be aware of the current situation and focus on your most dangerous opponent.

Also take into account that each of the possible dice rolls between two and twelve have a different probability of appearing. Numbers in the vicinity of seven will be relatively common, whereas the highest and lowest results will be pretty rare.

....

? Question 5

....

Probability of particular values: What is, on average, the percentage of your rolls resulting in a sum between five and nine? How many times during a game can you expect a roll of eleven or twelve?

Variant: Multego

This "lone warrior variant" for Catego offers less conflict and also the possibility of a one-player game:

This version relies less on the best result in a particular column and more on getting the highest total score. For this purpose, multiply your result with the point value of the corresponding column during each round, and record this value in your scoring row. Whoever has the highest total points in their row at the end of the game, wins.

At most, by only rolling twelves, it is possible to score 924 points. The luck of the dice is important in all this. If you want to reduce the amount of luck involved, you can only make one roll per round which now counts for everyone and is entered one after the other by the players into the column of their choice. The dice will go from one player to the next after each round, so that every turn a different player starts by entering their result.

It is not possible to affect other players in this variant. In that respect, you will find this is a somewhat calmer game which you can also play on your own. However, in a multiplayer game it is about keeping track of your opponents. This will determine your strategies and allow you to adapt the risks you take to the current situation.

Four by Four

Number of Players: 1 to 4
Length: 10 minutes per player
Components: 4 dice, score sheets

Components:

We need four dice and the score sheet below for *each* player:

	X 1	X 2	X 3	X 4
1				
2				
3				
4				

Game Concept:

The players take turns rolling the dice and recording their result in one of the free spaces in their score sheets. In the process, they have to decide whether to score the ones, twos, threes or fours, and whether the result will be counted once, twice, three times, or even four times. A roll with a five or six is not worth any points. Whoever has the most points at the end wins the game.

Setup:

Agree in which order you will play and give each player their own score sheet.

Gameplay:

The game takes place over 16 rounds, during which all players will take their turns one after the other.

During your turn, begin by throwing all four dice. After each of your rolls, you have to keep at least one of your dice, the others can be re-rolled. Dice that have been kept once cannot be re-rolled again. After four rolls at most, you will have your result. If the final roll of your turn contains a five or a six, the point value of the entire turn is zero.

Now, you will have to decide into which free space on your score sheet you want to record your result. For an invalid roll—one that contains a five or a six—you have to cross out a space of your choice. Apart from that, in the first row only the ones count, in the second only the twos, in the third only the threes and in the fourth only the fours. Therefore, depending on which row you choose, determine the sum of all valid dice.

Now, depending on which position you choose in the row, the sum will count once, twice, thrice or even quadruple and enter this result in the corresponding space.

Let us assume your first roll has the following outcome:

Apparently, it would be worthwhile to go with the threes. Therefore, you keep the two threes and roll the other two dice again:

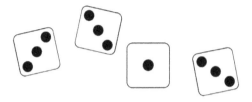

Now you have three threes in total. We can re-roll the last die and hope for another three. The risk of ruining the whole roll by getting a five or six is pretty high, though. Therefore, you decide to keep this result. With this, you have scored a sum of nine for the third row. As the chances of ever getting four threes are fairly small, it is advisable to choose the highest scoring with this result. Multiply it by four and record the 36 points in the last column:

	X 1	X 2	X 3	X 4
1				
2				
3				36
4				

36																

In order to keep track of the game's progress, you should use the row at the bottom to record your current cumulative total score.

Game end:

After 16 rounds, each player's score sheet will be filled completely, ending the game.

If you used the bottom row to keep track of your score, the last space will now contain the total score of each player. The player with the highest total score wins the game.

Game tactics:

It is possible to reach a total of 400 points. The fourth row alone could be worth 160 points, whereas the first row pales somewhat in comparison with only 40. Therefore, it could pay off to try and optimize your rolls for the higher rows while disregarding the first or even the second. Even then, it is all about balance, as in the end, every point you score will count for the victory.

It will require finesse to distribute your rolls most efficiently throughout the course of the whole game. Don't expect too much from your last couple of turns. Take your chances while you still have them.

Suggestions

The concept of category games gives us many starting points for other interesting games. As a start, you could change the game play in such a way that the various categories can't just be used once, but improved and overwritten any number of times. Then, the game doesn't take place over a fixed amount of rounds, but ends when a player has filled all of their categories. If you award a bonus for completely filling your score sheet, your dilemma between improving weak scores and the race for finishing the sheet first will increase steadily.

You also don't have to limit the components to the standard dice used here. You can vary the dice, paste over the sides with colored symbols and create completely new categories based on colors, shapes and symbols. Or use cards instead, or even completely different components. Develop your own game – the possibilities are virtually endless!

CHANCELLOR

Now we enter the world of politics. The struggle for votes and political mandates begins here. No other theme is more appropriate for negotiation games.

First of all, it is about placing the candidates and giving them the support they need. Then, everything depends on communicating, bargaining, making the right decisions quickly, and persuading the other players.

Constantly shifting coalitions are needed in order to succeed in the constant struggle for power. Having the better cards then becomes less important. Now, only coalition agreements, persuasion skills, and assertiveness counts.

Demonstrate your political skills!

Chancellor

Number of Players: 3 to 5
Length: 20 minutes per single game
Components: 2 decks of 52 cards

Game Concept:

In politics, an elected candidate receives a "mandate"—the authority granted by the voters to act as its representative. The goal is to get elected and, perhaps, to attain the ultimate position of Chancellor. After that, your goal is that of any other politician—to stay in power!

The players will try to win at least one candidate card and as many vote cards as possible in the various suits. Each suit represents a different state. This happens over many rounds in which the players take turns displaying cards from their hands in front of themselves.

Each time a player takes a turn, they first check for suits where they currently display more power than any opponent. In this case, the player wins these cards from their own display. All other players must discard their cards of the corresponding suits. In this way, the players compete simultaneously in all four suits, winning some of their own displayed cards and losing others to more powerful opponents - always under pressure to keep the upper hand in the struggle for power.

After all cards have been played, the players with the majority of votes will provide the individual Prime Ministers (in each state) and the overall Chancellor. In the next game, the players will receive individual bonus cards for their current mandates. Power leads to more power... Points will be awarded for votes as well as for the political mandates. Whoever has the most points after multiple games wins.

Components: We need two standard decks of 52 cards.

The cards from Two to Ten are "vote cards". All vote cards have a value of 1, regardless of their actual numeric value.

The Jack, Queen, and Kings are called "candidate cards". The Jacks have a value of 2, the Queens a value of 3, and the Kings a value of 4.

Depending on the number of players, we will use a different stack of cards:

Number of players	3	4	5
Vote cards of each suit	all 2 to 10 cards from one deck (36 cards)	all 2 to 7 from two decks (48 cards)	all 2 to 8 cards from two decks (56 cards)
Candidate cards of each suit	all Jacks, Queens, and Kings from two decks (24 cards)		
Total number of cards	60	72	80
Number of cards per player	20	18	16

Setup: Agree on the number of single games you want to play, for example four. Create the stack of cards as listed above and shuffle it well. Distribute the cards equally among all players and determine the starting player.

Gameplay:

The players take turns one after the other. In the first round, each player must play one or more of their hand cards and display them face-up in front of themselves. That's all that happens in the first round. Subsequent rounds start the process of evaluation, trick-taking (when possible), and playing one or more additional cards.

When it is your turn again, begin by evaluating your own displayed card or cards to see if you have a higher total value than each of your opponents in any of the suits. Remember, each vote card (number card) is worth 1 point.

The candidate cards (face cards) are worth the following: Jack = 2; Queen = 3; and King = 4.

If your card or cards have the highest value, you win all cards of this suit from your own display. (You can only win your own cards.) All other players will lose their displayed cards of the same suit and they are put in the discard pile.

The cards you won are put aside face-up. These will only be of significance during scoring at the end of the game. This must be done with all the cards you win, even if that would mean weakening your position for the future.

Afterwards, play one or more cards from your hand again, ending your turn. As long as you have any hand cards, you must play at least one card.

To make things simple and to easily monitor the progress of the game, you should organize the playing area as follows:

- In the center of the playing area, set up a face-down discard pile for the cards lost by the players. Players are not allowed to look at these cards.
- Place your cards that are currently in play at the side nearest to you in the vicinity of the discard pile. These will be sorted by suit.
- Place the cards you won in a separate area closest to yourself.

An important note: you may win two or more candidate cards of the same suit. You only need to keep one since additional candidate cards are of no significance (ultimately only one candidate per suit can hold office and they don't vote!). Also, the point value is not relevant to the selection of the Prime Minister and Chancellor, only the number of votes. Put any extra candidates of the same suit in the discard pile.

Here's an example of play. The following illustration is of a four person game in progress. You are the player at the bottom (the "South" position) and it is your turn.

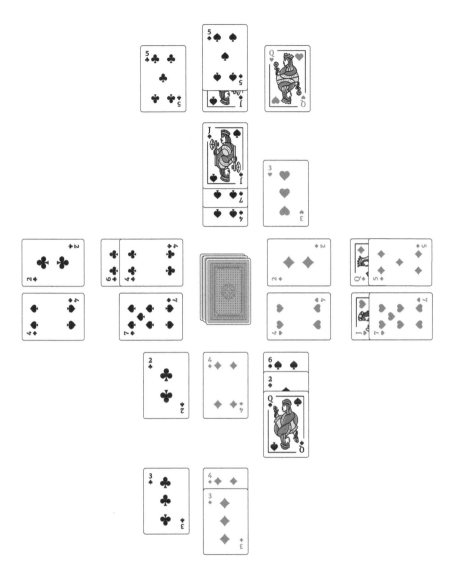

First, you evaluate the cards that are currently displayed. In this case, you win all Spade cards in your display.

- The player at the West position has a Spade displayed...a vote card with a value of 1.

- The player at North has three spades displayed...a Jack valued at 2 and two vote cards, each valued at 1 for a total value of 4.

- East has no Spades in active play.
- Your hand has a total value of 5 — one point each for the two spot cards plus 3 points for the Queen.

So...

- You take your own displayed Spades—the Queen and the two spot cards—and place them into your "cards won" area.
- West places his one Spade card into the discard pile.
- North places his three spade cards—the Jack and both spot cards—into the discard pile.

Your turn still isn't over. You continue to evaluate the other active cards, suit by suit.

- The Diamonds are tied at one each, as are the Hearts. There is no immediate need for action. You will certainly have another turn to react before any of those cards will be removed.
- You will lose your Club cards soon, however, if you don't play at least another card of the same suit. With two or more Clubs on display you will gain superiority and place the ball in your opponent's court.

Now it's time to complete your turn. If you still have cards remaining in your hand, you must play one or more of them. After that, play passes to the next player.

Game end:

When all hand cards have been played, the game continues until all possible card acquisitions have been made. Only then does the game end.

Cards that can't be won by any players due to ties go into the discard pile.

Scoring:

For each vote card you have won, you score 1 point. Now things start to get interesting! To start with:

- Players without candidate cards can neither be elected nor prevent a mandate, no matter how many vote cards they hold.
- Additionally, your candidate needs at least one vote card to receive a mandate, even if you are the only player with a suitable candidate card.
- In case of a tie, the mandate will not be awarded to any player.

First it is time for each state (each suit) to elect a Prime Minister (if possible). Each Prime Minister is worth 6 points.

In order to provide the Prime Minister for one of the four suits, you need to have:

- at least one candidate card (Jack, Queen, or King) in that suit;
- more vote cards in that **same** suit than any other player who also has a candidate card with the same suit.

Note: In this phase, the candidate cards have no point value. It is the number of votes received by a candidate that counts!

Once the Prime Ministers are elected, it's time to designate the Chancellor. The Chancellor is worth 12 points.

The player that has the highest total number of vote cards (the sum of your vote cards in all four suits) becomes Chancellor. Even here, the decision is made only between players with at least (any) one candidate card.

Let's have a look at the end game situation depicted below:

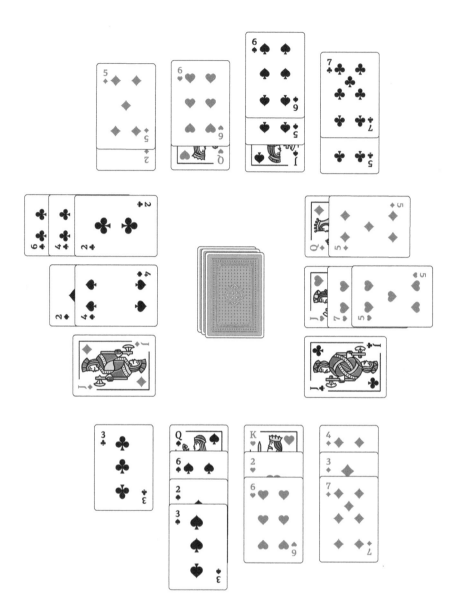

The first task is to identify the Prime Ministers:

- You (as the player towards the bottom or "South") can provide
  the Prime Minister in Spades. Your candidate has three votes,

compared to the next highest holding in Spades at the top (North position). That player only has two votes.

- Even though you hold the most votes in Diamonds, you will have to relinquish your right to the Prime Minister to the player on your right. Unfortunately, you have no candidate to carry those votes!

- No mandate will be awarded for Clubs. Three players have votes but no candidates. The player on your right has a candidate, but no votes.

- Hearts also has no Prime Minister. You are tied for votes with the player to your right. (Remember, in this phase the candidate cards have no point value. It's just about the number of votes.) In the case of a tie, no mandate is awarded.

Who's the Chancellor? Since you outmatch every other player with a total of nine votes (here you count only the number cards), you will become Chancellor. With your 12 point bonus for becoming Chancellor you will receive a total of 27 points. (6 points for becoming a Prime Minister of Spades plus 9 points for total votes plus 12 points for becoming Chancellor.) The player to your right gets nine points (6 points for becoming a Prime Minister of Diamonds plus 3 points for total votes.)

The remaining two players have no mandates and only reach five and seven points based on their number cards (votes).

After you have played the number of single games you agreed on beforehand, the player with the highest total score wins the game.

Bonus cards: All members of parliament will receive a bonus in the subsequent game: the player who provided the Chancellor will receive a King in all four suits for their hand cards before shuffling the deck. All other players (except the Chancellor) will at least receive a King for each Prime Minister of the corresponding suit. (Keep in mind that there are two Kings of each suit in the game.)

All players will start the next game with the same number of hand cards again, so distribute the cards accordingly, keeping in mind the bonus cards that have been awarded earlier and they count toward the total number of cards in any individual's hand.

Game tactics: At the beginning of each single game, you should make a brief analysis of your hand cards and think about which goals you can expect to reach. Keep in mind that you will only be able to win your own cards. Then, pursue your goals consistently and try to block your opponents accordingly.

In a four-player game, for any given suit there are two Kings (8 points), two Queens (6 points), two Jacks (4 points) and two runs of the spot (vote) cards 2 through 7 (12 points) for a total of 30 points. With the hand cards pictured below, you should have no problems to obtain the Prime Minister in Clubs.

From the total value of 30, you alone are in possession of 13. Initially, you should try and win a Jack in order to add additional vote cards afterwards. This way, you won't need to fear the two Kings later on, when you have already partially used up your hand and only have to defend your voting majority. Should the Kings appear early, leave them be and build up your majority afterwards without any resistance.

In Spades, you also have strong candidate cards at your disposal, though the very weak support with only one vote card will require a sophisticated approach in order to win the Prime Minister in addition to the single point for the vote card. Don't expect to be able to successfully block all the vote cards, but instead focus on blocking the other three candidate cards. Don't spring into action yourself, but let your opponents make the first move.

Inversely, you would have a sufficient voting potential with Diamonds, but without a candidate you won't be able to have a mandate. Try to win at least a few votes in this situation and don't try to take on any of the other players.

With Hearts, you won't be able to gain any points directly with the cards you have. Therefore, you should use your two candidate cards to force a tie with that suit or weaken the chances of your fiercest opponent at chancellorship, especially towards the end of the game.

Playing your cards at the right moment can decide a game. By default, you should play single vote cards in order not to squander your strong candidate cards unnecessarily.

If you encounter opposition by other players when playing your cards, you will have to decide quickly if it makes more sense to let yourself be dragged into an extended conflict, only to possibly lose everything at the end, or if you would prefer to backtrack before too many cards are involved. Sometimes, you might be able to bring someone to their knees by letting a portion of their cards pass unhindered, until their hand cards (through discards and fighting other players) are sufficiently weakened and strike during the decisive tussle.

If at all possible, you should usually only play one card per round. Otherwise you will lose your hand cards too early and you will then have no more opportunity to react during the last couple of rounds. The final stage of the game often brings a considerable shift in power in the various suits.

Variant: Cabinet

In contrast to the regular game, you can also agree that instead of the sole assignment of the Chancellor, a whole cabinet will be formed. Then, in the fight for chancellorship, only the vote cards of a suit for which the player also has a candidate card count. (The Chancellor can only count on votes in a suit for which they could win a candidate for their cabinet.)

Whoever becomes Chancellor will also only receive Kings as bonus cards during the next game for which they had at least one candidate.

Tactics-wise, the chancellorship can now be influenced more easily than before. For your own success, in addition to winning votes, it now depends primarily on blocking opposing cabinet members and enabling your own efforts.

As an additional intensification of this variant, you can also require a player to only be able to become Chancellor if they have won a candidate of each suit. The chancellorship will then only be decided between those players via the majority of votes.

Variant: Parliament

If you allow any kind of deal and negotiations and award the points for the mandates based on coalition negotiations, this will take Chancellor to an entirely new level.

In this variant, the game will no longer give you any points for vote cards alone.

In order to provide a Prime Minister, you will now need at least one candidate card of the relevant suit and, additionally, the support of the absolute majority of all vote cards of that suit that players have won. Accordingly, the Chancellor (with at least one candidate card) will now be elected with the absolute majority of all vote cards won by players. For wining those elections, you will again receive six and twelve points, respectively.

In order to obtain the required support, you can offer some of the points gained with a mandate to other players. However, other side payments are not possible, and the bonus cards are only available to the members of the parliament.

Alternatively, you can also play this variant by establishing a whole cabinet instead of only the Chancellor. Exactly one candidate of each suit has to belong to the cabinet. They have to agree on the distribution of the mandate points and have to be confirmed by holding the absolute majority of all vote cards won by players. Aside from the bonus cards for the Prime Ministers, all players will also receive a King of the suits of their cabinet members.

If no agreement can be reached on an individual decision, the corresponding mandate will not be assigned.

You can be sure that in this variant, after all cards have been played, there will be hot debates over the mandates, as a single player will only have the absolute majority in the very rarest cases. Consider what might be happening in a single suit as depicted in the following endgame situation:

SEE NEXT PAGE

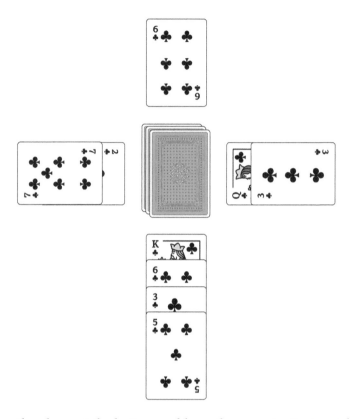

You are the player at the bottom and have the opportunity to establish a coalition with each of the other players. As a result, you can play the other players off against each other, in order to avoid handing over too many points. If you go overboard, however, you run into the danger of the other players establishing a coalition without you.

Apparently, the player towards your right is in a relatively strong position, as he alone is in possession of the candidate required for that coalition and therefore would be sure to receive the associated bonus card. The player towards your left, on the other hand, could insist on the significant contribution of their two vote cards and gain a majority of the mandate points as a result.

The weakest player (on top) with just one vote also wants to be compensated fairly for their required approval to the coalition. Therefore, an agreement about the distribution of the coalition winnings (six points and the bonus card) won't be easy, especially since you will do everything in your power to win another player to your side. The weakest player might possibly be your best bet for that option.

During negotiations, you should keep the order of the parliament: first, the Prime Ministers will be elected in the sequence of the suits: Clubs, Spades, Hearts, and Diamonds. Only afterwards will you make a binding agreement and decide the Chancellor and the composition of the cabinet. Before every single vote, determine the number of required votes for the mandate. Right after the decision, record the awarded points and bonus cards. This can't be changed later on in the game.

Tactics-wise, you should prepare yourself for the later coalition negotiations when initially playing your cards. When a player has already won a candidate and multiple vote cards in one suit, it is beneficial for your own chances at negotiation to avert an opponent's absolute majority even by supporting your opponent's vote cards. If you succeed in another way to block all opposing candidates of a suit, you will inevitably play a part in the formation of the cabinet.

Variant: Democracy

In order to experience the whole repertoire of politics, you can play with open hands during your turns already and, due to the added transparency of all information, start with the negotiations from the very beginning: who's helping whom and which services does he receive in return?

As a modification to the prior game play, it can now be very exciting by introducing the rule that a player can also win the displayed cards of their opponents in addition to their own, making the discard pile unnecessary.

As you, of course, can't win all your hand cards for yourself, it will now depend on which player will receive your remaining cards. The later balance of power in the parliament can be greatly influenced that way. Secure the promise of points in the following parliamentary debate as your reward.

Suggestions

Politics thrives on the diversity of opinions. In this sense, you can expand the game to be played with more than five players:

The only thing you need to do for this is to create a special deck of cards with more than four suits – the game play itself doesn't have to be changed much, if at all. With simple and clear components the game will still be determined by the group dynamics anyway.

DESK-JOGGING

Marathon is an ancient city on the east coast of Attica. Here, the Athenian ground forces under the command of Miltiades defeated the Persians in 490 BC as a result of his superior tactics. We all know the story of a runner who brought the news of victory into Athens, 42 kilometers from where he started and subsequently collapsed from exhaustion and died. Thus the marathon was born.

Today, running is a widespread and popular sport. In order to be successful during the training and the race itself, it is all about pacing yourself well. Whoever starts too slowly will not win the race, just like the athlete who wears himself out too early may never even reach the finish line.

In the following dice game, you will also have to use your chances effectively in order to be one step ahead of your competitors at the end!

Desk-Jogging

Number of Players: 1 to 4
Length: 5 minutes per player
Components: 4 dice

Game Concept: The players take turns rolling the dice and dividing them into anywhere from one to four groups. The sum of each individual group has to increase with every new roll. Whoever reaches a total sum of 100 points first wins the game.

Components: We need 4 dice and something to write with.

Setup: Agree about the order you want the competitors to play and reserve two lines for each player on your notepad. All players start with a score of zero.

Gameplay: The players take turns one after the other. When it is your turn, roll all four dice and pick at least one of them, which cannot not be re-rolled. Afterwards, you can re-roll all other dice, but after each roll at least one new die has to be kept. Dice which are kept this way cannot be re-rolled again. After four rolls (at most) you have your result:

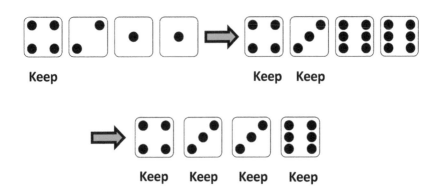

Keep   Keep   Keep

Keep   Keep   Keep   Keep

In the previous example each subsequent roll is marked with an arrow.

Then, arrange the four dice into one to four groups. Each die can only be used once this way. The sum of each group has to be greater than the one before it and therefore all have to be different:

Total = 3   **Total = 6**   **Total = 7**

To end your turn, determine the total of all dice values and add it as your score, recording it on the first line of the notepad. Below it, also record the highest sum of your groups. It should look like this:

16
7

Starting with the second round, the sum of your current roll has to be higher than the highest sum in your previous turn (indicated on the second line)."

If these requirements are not met, the roll is invalid and will not be added to your score. You are also allowed to declare a roll as invalid if it is technically valid, but undesirable for you.

Based on the current score, your largest group must be 8 or higher. The final result of your next turn is:

Total = 8   **Total = 9**

When you produce a valid result, determine the sum of your four dice again and add it to your previous score. Record the new total score on your notepad and also write down the highest sum from your groups of your current roll below it:

16   33
7   9

After this, your turn ends and the next player will take theirs.

Game end:

When a player reaches a score of 100 or more points, the current round will be finished, however the other players are allowed to continue until each player has had an equal number of turns. Afterwards, the game ends.

Then, the player with the highest total score wins. In case of a tie you must roll the dice to determine who wins. The places of the other players are determined by their scores.

In a one player game, it is your goal to reach 100 points with the least number of rolls.

Game tactics:

Does the game appear as too simplistic and mostly dependent on luck? After the first few rounds you will realize that there is plenty of opportunity for tactical choices there are numerous ways to control the outcome.

You want to reach 100 points as quickly as possible! As a result, you shouldn't jog too slowly. A low roll will slow you down, no matter how you will arrange it into groups. Therefore, you should try to avoid the Ones and Twos as much as possible.

Then again, don't start too quickly, as there is nothing worse than wearing yourself down before the finishing line and having to watch helplessly as you are overtaken one by one by the other players. If you start out too slowly, you lose a few points, but if you start too quickly, you will lose the game. That's the big risk!

Be careful and make sure that the sums in the groups don't increase too rapidly. Arranging the dice into the right groups can make or break a game: only during the first round do you have the opportunity to make four groups with just a single die each. It is especially advantageous if you can make do with groups of two dice in the second and third round and only use a group of four dice during the fourth round. This way, you can leave half of the track behind yourself before you even have to use a group of four.

The lowest group sum achievable is a 3. (If you roll four ones, you have a group of one die worth 1 and a group of three dice worth 3. Remember, the sum of each group has to be greater than the one before it and therefore all have to be different.) The highest group sum achievable is 24. That is done by rolling four sixes and combining them into one group of four dice.

If you go into the unwieldy groups of four too quickly and without having a sufficient buildup of points, you will have to slow down to still be able to fit in all the rolls you need to reach your goal. As you can't exactly control every single roll you make, you will always have the risk of getting very high rolls (around 20), which will cause many invalid rolls and cost you many rounds.

Especially during the second half, you should be aware of the steps needed to reach the finish line:

16   33   55
7   9   12

For example, in the situation pictured above, you can't really expect to reach the goal with fewer than three steps. Therefore, it wouldn't be very wise in this situation to accept a roll with a sum higher than 20. After this burst, you would have to get two more high rolls and that is risky and may take a lot of time. Being able to have around 120 points still won't help you much if another player was faster than you. It is much more reasonable to safely trot towards the goal with a pace of around 14 points per round.

You can practice a little by playing the game on your own. The experience of a few games will help you to plan future runs more effectively.

Variant: Versatility-Jogging

Aside from the regular distance of 100 points, you can also choose longer routes with 120 points, for example. Then it is even more important to start slowing pace yourself effectively.

Instead of a fixed distance, you can also use a limited number of rounds, such as eight or ten. At the end, the player with the highest number of points wins. As every invalid roll will cost you valuable points, you will have to find the right tempo based on the number of rounds.

Another possible variant neither uses a fixed distance nor a limited number of rounds, but considers an invalid roll as the player's end of the run. After each player has ended their run with an invalid roll, the player who came farthest and consequently has the most points wins the game.

One way to increase the intensity of the previous variant is to regard an invalid roll as a stop marker which disqualifies a player. Then, you will have to decide on your own to stop your run early enough. At the end, the player who has a valid run and scored the most points wins the game. Disqualified players are disregarded. The risk of being disqualified makes this variant particularly exciting.

Finally, you can also look only at the number of completed rounds. Ending your run on your own is not possible anymore. Each player with an invalid roll is out of the game. In case of a tie, the player with the higher score wins. Besides that, the points are not important any longer. Whoever can run the longest wins the game. Of course, you will have to start as slowly as possible here.

With all of these different variants you could even plan a jogging championship with all the various races held one after the other. In such a tournament each contestant can prove their versatility. Offer some prize money for the first few places and whoever has collected the most prize money at the end will be declared the champion.

Variant: Obstacle-Jogging

In this variant, each turn costs ten points, which will be subtracted from the result of the roll. You can play as many rounds as you wish. It makes sense to end your run at a reasonable time, though, before the obstacles become too big to handle and cause you to reduce your score with invalid rolls. Once you have passed and skipped a turn, you also won't be able to resume your run again later on.

Here, it all depends on having as many rolls as possible in order to have a sum greater than ten and then choosing the best time to stop your run. It is also advisable to start very slowly in order to stay in the game as long as possible which could allow you to dominate the end game.

Variant: Relay-Jogging

All previous variants can be expanded by having a run consist of multiple stages, during which the sum of the groups start at zero again, but the total score is recorded as usual.

For that matter, it is not required that all players switch to the next stage in the same round. Or you could decide to allow the transition to the next stage to happen automatically after an invalid roll, or leave the decision up to the individual players. In this case, the players have to announce that they are starting a new stage before they roll the dice.

A typical example for relay-jogging would be a run for 300 points over three stages.

Suggestions

You are also free to use more dice when playing with any and all variants of Desk-Jogging. The importance of creating the right groups is increased by this approach.

If you have a large number of players you can – especially when using more dice – completely disregard all the calculations and the total scores and instead only focus on the positions of the players themselves. For example, try to flesh out the following idea into a complete game:

Each player will use a playing piece with their name. The points resulting from the first round determines the order and you can arrange the pieces accordingly. Here, only the order of the individual runners counts and not the distance between them.

During successive rounds, turns will be made in order, starting with the player in first place, followed by the second and so on. If you score more points during your turn than the player in front of yourself, you can overtake them and put your piece ahead of theirs. While doing so, you can only get one step ahead.

The game is over when, during a complete round, no player has changed their position. Then, the current positions are the final places of the individual players.

EXCURSION INTO COMBINATORICS

All of you probably know the story about the ruler who wants to greatly reward a subject for a rendered service. The subject replies: "Put a single grain of rice on the first space of a chess board, two grains on the second, four grains on the third, and double the number of grains each time until you reach the 64th space. Let this be my reward."

The sultan was overjoyed over this apparently very modest wish, as the servant would have been worth his weight in gold. Carelessly, he agreed.

What the sultan didn't know: due to the grains being doubled with each space, the number of the required grains grew so big that the rice harvest of the entire world would not have been enough to fill it.

Sometimes, it doesn't hurt to be able to count and calculate a little. This will be our topic for this chapter.

Excursion into Combinatorics

M uch of the fun in games involving dice and cards comes from the fact that you can't know for certain what the next roll of the dice will bring or what the next draw of the cards will show. Sometimes we can make a "best guess", but this is really in the form of what is more or less likely to happen on this turn. While it's not certain, it may be enough to guide you toward a winning strategy. This chapter is rather technical and is here for those individuals who would like an insight into what goes on to make such a game different each time we play it, and to give you an idea as to what is possible, probable, or unlikely as the cards flip or the dice roll. Those of you who hated mathematics when you were in school might find this chapter a bit daunting and you can skip ahead to the next game. You'll still be able to understand the mechanics of the play without worrying about the underlying probabilities and combinations.

Mathematical combinatorics deals with techniques of counting. It systematically explores how certain objects can be arranged given certain rules or principles. In the process it demonstrates that it is no longer necessary to count each case individually, and even this is be possible with more complex problems.

To be able to display our results independently from individual examples, we will use the letters m, n, and r instead of numbers, for which you can substitute natural numbers $(1, 2, 3, \ldots)$, depending on the situation.

Counting principle: We will start with a fundamental counting principle, which we will often refer to. We start off with two different types of objects and ask ourselves how many times we can combine an object of one type with an object of a different type.

Suppose we have *m* different objects of the first and *n* different objects of the second type. Each object of the first type can be combined with objects of the second type, so that we will get *m x n* different pairs. For m = 3 (A, B, C) and n = 4 (1, 2, 3, 4), we can make 12 different pairs:

	1	2	3	4
A	A 1	A 2	A 3	A 4
B	B 1	B 2	B 3	B 4
C	C 1	C 2	C 3	C 4

Counting principle: From m objects of a type and n objects of a different type exactly m x n different pairs can be created. Even with more than two types of objects, the number of possibilities is calculated by combining one object of each type with each other, forming the product of the number of objects of each type.

For example, the combination of 13 different card values (first type) with four different suits (second type) gives us our familiar deck of cards with 13 x 4 = 52 cards. With a rummy game of 2 x 52 cards, this stack of cards is also equipped with two different backs (third type).

Selection principles: To select exactly r pieces from m different objects, you could use fundamentally different selection principles:

It makes a big difference whether you can only pick each object once or if you also allow an object to be picked multiple times. Without duplicates the number of selections (r) can of course not be higher than the number of objects (m). Another complicating fact is whether the order in which the individual objects are picked is important, or whether the order of the objects doesn't matter. If the order doesn't matter then the selections 1 2 3 4 and 2 3 4 1 are the same, but if order is important then they are not.

A typical example for each of these selection principles can be found in the table below. (The objects which have to be kept track of are in parenthesis.)

Selection	ordered (the order is important)	unordered (the order is not important)
without duplicates of the same objects	placings in a horse-race (horse)	lottery "6 from 49" (lottery number)
with duplicates of the same objects	football pools (game result)	dice throws (numbers on each die)

In a horse-race, each horse can only finish once, and the order is important. In a lottery too, each number can only be drawn once, though the order the numbers are drawn in is not important. When betting on soccer pools, you will bet on individual game results, which don't have to be different. However, it is not only about the results of the individual games, but also about how you assign the results to the individual games. (When you swap two game results, it will make a difference.) When throwing several dice you also can have the same number twice. However the order in which the dice fall on the table is irrelevant.

Each selection principle requires different counting techniques, which we will now go into:

Ordered selection without duplicates: In how many ways can we select exactly r pieces (one after the other) from m different objects, if each object can only be picked once and the order of the chosen objects is important?

Obviously, we have m possibilities when choosing the first object. Afterwards, we only have m-1 options left for the second object. With every new choice, the number of our objects will be decreased, so that we can ultimately choose the rth object only from m-r+1 alternatives. With this counting principle we will arrive at the following conclusion:

Ordered selection without duplicates: From m different objects, r objects can be selected in exactly m x (m-1) x (m-2) x . . . x (m-r+1) different ways.

(Each object can only be picked once. The order of the chosen objects is important.)

The question of the different results in a horse-race can now be answered quite easily. For example, if eight horses participate in the race, there are 8 x 7 x 6 = 336 different possibilities for the places of the first three horses.

To solve the same problem by merely counting all possible cases, we would have to create the somewhat elaborate table below. (The individual horses are numbered from 1 to 8.) Given the combinatorial principles this is not necessary anymore.

123	162	231	271	341	381	451	512	561	621	671	731	781	841
124	163	234	273	342	382	452	513	562	623	672	732	782	842
125	164	235	274	345	384	453	514	563	624	673	734	783	843
126	165	236	275	346	385	456	516	564	625	674	735	784	845
127	167	237	276	347	386	457	517	567	627	675	736	785	846
128	168	238	278	348	387	458	518	568	628	678	738	786	847
132	172	241	281	351	412	461	521	571	631	681	741	812	851
134	173	243	283	352	413	462	523	572	632	682	742	813	852
135	174	245	284	354	415	463	524	573	634	683	743	814	853
136	175	246	285	356	416	465	526	574	635	684	745	815	854
137	176	247	286	357	417	467	527	576	637	685	746	816	856
138	178	248	287	358	418	468	528	578	638	687	748	817	857
142	182	251	312	361	421	471	531	581	641	712	751	821	861
143	183	253	314	362	423	472	532	582	642	713	752	823	862
145	184	254	315	364	425	473	534	583	643	714	753	824	863
146	185	256	316	365	426	475	536	584	645	715	754	825	864
147	186	257	317	367	427	476	537	586	647	716	756	826	865
148	187	258	318	368	428	478	538	587	648	718	758	827	867
152	213	261	321	371	431	481	541	612	651	721	761	831	871
153	214	263	324	372	432	482	542	613	652	723	762	832	872
154	215	264	325	374	435	483	543	614	653	724	763	834	873
156	216	265	326	375	436	485	546	615	654	725	764	835	874
157	217	267	327	376	437	486	547	617	657	726	765	836	875
158	218	268	328	378	438	487	548	618	658	728	768	837	876

In how many different ways can you roll different numbers with four differently colored dice? Here, we select four numbers between one and six with the help of the dice. As the individual dice can be distinguished from each other, we are now in a situation with an ordered selection. (Which die shows which number does make a difference.) The requirement of different numbers rules out any duplicates, so that we can apply the above formula, which results in 6 x 5 x 4 x 3 = 360 different cases.

r = m is an interesting special case, in which all objects are selected:

Evidently, m different objects can be arranged in exactly m x (m-1) x . . . x 2 x 1 different ways. To simplify the notation, we set m! = m x (m-1) x . . . x 2 x 1 and read m! as "m factorial". With an increasing m, m! will grow large very quickly.

For example, there are 52! = 52 x 51 x . . . x 2 x 1 different possibilities of how a standard deck of 52 cards can be shuffled. The calculation of this product results in an exceptionally high number with 68 digits. In a sufficiently shuffled deck of cards there is a very high probability that you can expect the exact same order of the 52 cards has never occurred anywhere on Earth before.

Now we may even be able to solve what may be the most well-known problem on a chess board very easily:

....

❓ Question 6

....

Eight rooks: How many different ways are there to arrange eight rooks on a chess board so that they are not able to capture each other?

(Consider that rooks can capture horizontally as well as vertically on the 8 x 8 board and each rook therefore has to be in a different column. When filling the columns you can use each of the eight rows exactly once.)

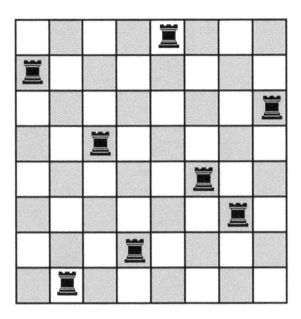

Unordered selection without duplicates: In how many ways can we choose exactly r pieces from m different objects, if each object can only be chosen once and the order of the chosen objects is not important?

We already know that there are m x (m-1) x ... x (m-r+1) different ordered possibilities. However, we don't want to distinguish between possibilities which only differ by the order of their objects any longer. As r objects can be arranged in r! = r x (r-1) x ... x 2 x1 different ways, there are exactly r! times as many ordered as unordered selections:

Unordered selection without duplicates: From m different objects, r objects can be chosen in exactly m x (m-1) x (m-2) x . . . x (m-r+1)/r! different ways. (Each object can only be chosen once. The order of the selected objects is of no importance.)

How many games, for instance, are to be held in a chess tournament with twelve participants, if each player has to play against every other player? Here, it is apparently about selecting two different players (without duplicates) and without considering the order ("A plays against B" is equal to "B plays against A"). With the formula we just derived we determine that there will be exactly 12 x 11/2! = 66 games.

Many combinatorial problems can be expressed by drawing lots from an urn. The lottery is typical for this:

There are 49 (numbered) balls in an urn, from which six are individually drawn without considering their order. For the outcome of the drawing there are a total of 49 x 48 x 47 x 46 x 45 x 44/6! = 13983816 different possibilities, as per our formula.

Now, let us also imagine that six of the 49 balls are black and the other 43 are white. (The black numbers correspond to the numbers on our lottery ticket.) Obviously, there is exactly one possible drawing among the 13983816 possibilities in which all of our six black balls are drawn. But in how many cases can we count on the lesser prize categories, such as five, four or three black balls?

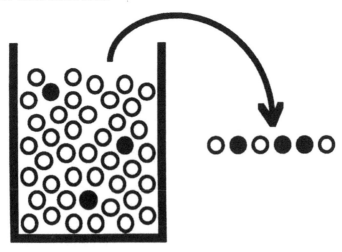

From the six black balls, five can be initially chosen in exactly 6 x 5 x 4 x 3 x 2/5! = 6 different ways. (One of the six balls will always stay behind.) For the selection of a white ball, there are now only 43 possibilities left. Considering the counting principle, there are 6 x 43 = 258 different drawings with exactly five black balls as a result.

In order to have exactly four matches in a drawing, we can draw four black balls in 6 x 5 x 4 x 3/4! = 15 and two white balls in exactly 43 x 42/2! = 903 different ways. In total, this provides us with 15 x 903 = 13545 cases. Finally, for the selection of three black and three white balls there are 6 x 5 x 4/3! = 20 and 43 x 42 x 41/3! = 12341 possibilities, respectively, which together result in 20 x 12341 = 246820 drawings with exactly three black balls.

Apparently, in unordered selections without duplicates we find ourselves in the typical situation of card games. Each card can only be given to a player once, and the order of the hand cards of each individual player is not important to the game.

 Question 7

Poker I: We are playing Poker, using a deck with 32 cards. (The cards have four different suits with eight different values each.) Each player initially receives five cards.

1. How many different combinations of cards can each player receive? (Choose five cards from 32.)
2. How many of these combinations consist of five different card values? (Begin by choosing five of the eight card values, and then consider that there are four different cards per card value.) How many combinations have at least one pair (two cards with the same value)?
3. How often do triplets (three with the same value) or quadruplets (four with the same value) occur? (Begin by determining all possible combinations with three and four Queens, respectively. Reference the urn model.)
4. How common are five cards of the same suit? (Begin by analyzing Hearts, and choose five of these eight cards again.)
5. How many combinations consist of five cards in sequence, and how often are they of the same suit?

(Determine in how many different ways you can combine the required card values and how many choices you then still have with each value.)

Ordered selection with duplicates: In how many different ways can we select exactly r pieces (one after the other) from m different objects, when individual objects can be selected multiple times and the order of the chosen objects is important?

Here, we have m options with each step, so that the counting principle now offers us this solution:

Ordered selection with duplicates: We can select r objects from m different objects in exactly m x m x ... x m (r times) different ways. (The individual objects can be chosen multiple times. The order of the chosen objects is important.)

For example, betting on soccer pools is all about predicting the outcome (victory, draw, or defeat) of eleven soccer games. The objects we have to consider are the three different outcomes here, from which we will select our choice eleven times in a row. Of course it is important to assign the choices of the different games in the right order, with some results inevitably appearing more than once. With the formula above we determine that there are 3 x 3 x 3 x 3 x 3 x 3 x 3 x 3 x 3 x 3 x 3 = 177147 different possibilities.

Only one of these possibilities will correctly predict the outcome of all games. When making exactly one mistake, there are apparently eleven different games and two wrong results for each to choose from, so that there are 11 x 2 = 22 bets with exactly ten correct predictions, according to the counting principle. In order to not have a single outcome correct, all eleven games each offer two incorrect outcomes, which we can combine to a total of 2 x 2 x 2 x 2 x 2 x 2 x 2 x 2 x 2 x 2 x 2 = 2048 of completely wrong bets.

How many different outcomes can a roll of four (differently colored) dice have? As opposed to our earlier example, the different dice can now show the same number. As each die can give one of six different results, we determine that there are 6 x 6 x 6 x 6 = 1296 different outcomes in total.

Many typical examples for ordered selections with duplicates happen as a result of applying the same random processes multiple times. While doing this, it is of no importance if the duplicates happen one after the other or at the same time.

 Question 8

Coin toss I: A coin is flipped ten times. How many different outcomes can this experiment have? How many times will we get exactly five heads and five tails? (In the second part of the question, answer in how many different ways we can select exactly five of the ten coins.)

Unordered selection with duplicates: Now the only question that remains is in how many different ways we can select exactly r pieces from m different objects, when objects are allowed to be selected multiple times and the order of the objects is of no importance.

Answering this question is fairly complicated and will be carried out here without any explanation:

Unordered selection with duplicates: We can select r objects from m different objects in exactly (m+r-1) x (m+r-2) x (m+r-3) x . . . x m/r! different ways. (The individual objects can be selected multiple times. The order of the chosen objects is of no importance.)

With this formula, we can for example very easily calculate how many different dominoes there are with numbers ranging from zero to six. While doing so, we will also allow dominoes which have the same number twice, but otherwise, the order of the two numbers on the domino is of no importance. In total, there are seven numbers from which we will choose the individual pairs. With m = 7 and r = 2, this results in 8 x 7/2! = 28 different dominoes.

To conclude this chapter, we will now get back to the roll with four different dice. This time, we don't differentiate between the individual dice any longer, but allow the same number to appear more than once.

Altogether, we choose four numbers between one and six with the help of the dice, resulting in 9 x 8 x 7 x 6/4! = 126 cases when disregarding the order. From the corresponding formula without duplicates, we realize that from these there are 6 x 5 x 4 x 3/4! = 15 cases where all the numbers are different.

In the following table, you will find a roundup of all possible rolls: firstly, you will find the 126 unordered rolls, from which 15 don't have any duplicates. Additionally, each roll lists the number of its possible orders, which gives us a view of all 1296 ordered rolls. 360 of these don't contain any duplicates.

01x	6666	04x	6555	24x	6431	12x	5542	12x	5322	24x	4321
04x	6665	12x	6554	12x	6422	12x	5541	24x	5321	12x	4311
04x	6664	12x	6553	24x	6421	06x	5533	12x	5311	04x	4222
04x	6663	12x	6552	12x	6411	12x	5532	04x	5222	12x	4221
04x	6662	12x	6551	04x	6333	12x	5531	12x	5221	12x	4211
04x	6661	12x	6544	12x	6332	06x	5522	12x	5211	04x	4111
06x	6655	24x	6543	12x	6331	12x	5521	04x	5111	01x	3333
12x	6654	24x	6542	12x	6322	06x	5511	01x	4444	04x	3332
12x	6653	24x	6541	24x	6321	04x	5444	04x	4443	04x	3331
12x	6652	12x	6533	12x	6311	12x	5443	04x	4442	06x	3322
12x	6651	24x	6532	04x	6222	12x	5442	04x	4441	12x	3321
06x	6644	24x	6531	12x	6221	12x	5441	06x	4433	06x	3311
12x	6643	12x	6522	12x	6211	12x	5433	12x	4432	04x	3222
12x	6642	24x	6521	04x	6111	24x	5432	12x	4431	12x	3221
12x	6641	12x	6511	01x	5555	24x	5431	06x	4422	12x	3211
06x	6633	04x	6444	04x	5554	12x	5422	12x	4421	04x	3111
12x	6632	12x	6443	04x	5553	24x	5421	06x	4411	01x	2222
12x	6631	12x	6442	04x	5552	12x	5411	04x	4333	04x	2221
06x	6622	12x	6441	04x	5551	04x	5333	12x	4332	06x	2211
12x	6621	12x	6433	06x	5544	12x	5332	12x	4331	04x	2111
06x	6611	24x	6432	12x	5543	12x	5331	12x	4322	01x	1111

SWAP

There are a number of economic games which are filled to the brim with various components: different game boards and reference cards, game pieces and dice, machines and commodities, play money and chips, event and market cards, stocks and properties – and plenty of special rules.

Throughout the course of the game you are preoccupied with organizing and keeping track of all the components. And so, you don't really get to "play" the game, despite the usually long playing time. There is a winner at the end, but often nobody really knows how this happened.

How pleasant the well-defined games are in contrast, those which can unfold a clear sector of business in front of your very eyes with only a few components. Freed from all trivialities you can actually focus on your game. The simplicity of the concept gives you a clear view of who makes the better decisions and who wins and why.

The following game simulates an extremely simple commodity market, in which you will generate earnings by buying and selling. The name of the game stems from the financial sector and refers to trades on the foreign exchange market.

Swap

Number of Players: 1 to 4
Length: 5 minutes per player
Components: 4 dice, 4 x 12 chips

Components: We need four (preferably same-colored) dice and four sets of 12 chips (or coins) in four different colors (or denominations).

Game idea: During each round, the dice are rolled to determine the four prices of the differently colored chips. All players try to use the price fluctuations to trade commodities in the most profitable ways. The first player to double their initial stock wins the game.

Setup: First, determine the order of the four colors from the most expensive to the least expensive. (We chose white, yellow, blue, and black.) Then, form the commodity market in the middle of the playing area by placing twice as many chips of each color, one below the other, as there are players, and place a die above each color. Give each player a chip of every color as initial stock and make sure that all inventory is clearly visible to everyone. While doing so, you should arrange the colors by their order. Then, agree on who begins.

The illustration following shows the initial setup for two players:

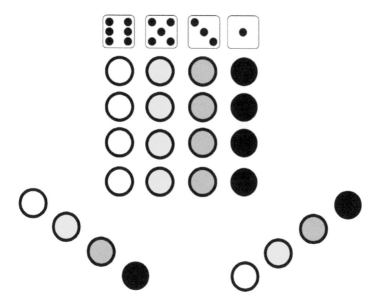

Gameplay: The first player rolls the four dice and sorts them by their numbers, so that the highest number is above the most expensive color and the lowest number is above the cheapest, thereby determining the prices for this round. Starting with the second player, the players now, one after the other, have the option of trading their chips on the commodity market. The first player, who rolled the dice, is the last to trade, which will conclude the round.

Afterwards, it's the second player's turn to begin the next round. They roll the dice for the new prices, sort them again by numbers and, after all other players have made their trades, concludes the round with their own trade. The game continues this way round after round.

Trading commodities: Each trade works the same way: you choose a number of your own chips to place on the commodity market. At the same time, you determine the value of the traded chips by adding the numbers on the dice above the corresponding colors. Afterwards, you can take chips from the market whose total value can't be higher than that of the chips you gave earlier. (Taking chips with lower value is also allowed.)

However, mind the following fundamental limitation on the market: you are only allowed to move one chip of each color throughout the whole exchange. At most, you can use a chip of one color and receive a chip or chips of the other colors.

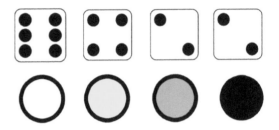

In the pictured price situation you could, for example, trade a white chip (with a value of 6) for a yellow and a blue chip (with the same value of 6):

Alternatively, the following options could also be interesting, considering the given prices:

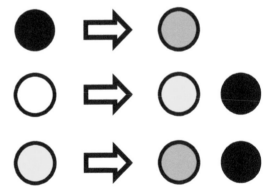

If, during the course of the game, a row is temporarily empty, then the corresponding commodity is currently not available on the market. If you are not able to find a suitable trade, you are not obligated to trade and can pass on trading for this turn instead.

Game end: The goal of the game is to double the initial stock of chips, meaning having at least two chips of each color. Whoever is the first player to do this wins the game. You can end the game there, or you can let the other players continue for the other places.

All players who can reach their goal during the same round will have to share their place, as they have traded the same number of times. (Meaning that here there can also be multiple winners with scores of equal value.) In one player swap, it is all about reaching the goal with the fewest number of trades as possible.

Game tactics: Of course you will try to buy when prices are low and sell when prices are high. Low and high doesn't refer to the absolute numbers on the dice, though, but to the price ratio of the colors towards each other. Therefore, you should disregard the numbers themselves and rather analyze which colors you can trade for each other. This way, you will end up with a much clearer assessment of the situation and avoid unreasonably trading back and forth without any increase in value.

 Question 9

Sensible swaps: Despite the huge number of possible rolls, there are only 20 reasonable trading options (swaps). Which options are these?

Often, you will have multiple reasonable options, from which you will have to make your decision based on your individual current situation. You should try to increase your value as much as possible during each turn, though towards the end it might also be sensible to make an unfavorable trade in order to reach the goal.

Average swap values: Try to calculate the expected average value for each of the four colors or at least make an educated guess. (If you would roll for each color individually, the average price of the numbers from one to six would be $(1 + 2 + 3 + 4 + 5 + 6)/6 = 3.5$. The situation here is noticeably more complicated, however!)

Use your result to calculate the average increase in value for each of the 20 swaps described in the previous question.

Aside from maximizing your increase in value, you should also try to have a well-balanced stock in order to keep your options open even during the later rounds. In the short-term, it is not only about increasing your value—particularly at the beginning of the game, you should try to increase your number of chips as quickly as possible.

As the individual players will barely affect each other, you can gather valuable experience during a one player game and get a sense of the swap relations. In how many turns can you reach your goal?

Variant: Sway Swap

Instead of having to play each round with constant prices, you can also let the prices fluctuate constantly by altering the game play slightly:

For this, you should roll the four dice once during the setup and arrange them by their numbers on the commodity market. During the course of the game, only individual dice will change.

Whenever it is a player's turn, they choose a die, roll it and place the die and the three others which weren't rolled on the commodity market, again sorted by their numbers. Then, the players have the opportunity to trade after which their turn ends. (Even if you don't want to trade you will have to roll a die regardless.) When this turn finishes the next player takes their turn.

Through this variant, you will have new options of influencing the price ratios, which you can now manipulate selectively. Of course, you should try to increase the prices of your own commodities while lowering those of the commodities you need. You should also keep track of your opponents' stocks in order to impede their progress.

As the placement of the dice is dependent on the numbers themselves, you can never be sure how the new number will actually influence the different colors. You will also find many more opportunities for strategic considerations. The one-player game here is also particularly exciting, because of this.

The difference here is that if all players roll all four dice instead of just one, there is no continuity in the market prices from one round to the next. Your options for deliberately manipulating the market are nil and luck has a substantial role in the game.

Variant: Sellout

A completely different way to change the game is separating the prices from the colors: do away with the orders of the colors and instead use dice with the same colors as the chips, which will now be permanently assigned to these colors.

Play the same way as in the previous variant where each player only changes a single die. Play, until the entire commodity market is completely sold out (and only has one chip left). Whoever has the most chips then wins the game.

Obviously, here it is all about increasing the number of chips as much as possible with each trade. Having a well-balanced stock portfolio is especially important, as each missed swap means less chips and as a consequence, maybe even defeat.

Suggestions

You can also expand the regular Swap or any of the variants to use five colors and five dice.

The concept of the game is not changed by this in any way, but it will open many more trading options. This turns out to be a variant for experienced players!

By changing the trading rules, you can give the game and its variants a whole new flavor. For example, allow trading any four (even same-colored) chips per turn, or completely abolish all limitations when trading chips.

Then, trading as many chips as possible is important to profit the most from the individual price increases. Shortages will play a much bigger role and sometimes you might even have to introduce special rules in order to not lock down a game completely.

If you also allow bilateral trade between players, you will head in the direction of a very complex economic game.

DUBITO

Do you know about the story of the mysterious Sphinx, whose monument still stands in Egypt today? Each traveler who passed her, she posed a riddle: "What creature walks on four legs in the morning, two legs at noon and three in the evening?" (The answer is "man"— in youth he crawls on all fours, in his prime he walks on two legs, and in old age he walks with the use of a cane.) Only those who knew the correct answer were allowed to proceed; those that answered incorrectly were devoured. Today, a similar concept is the basis of many "trivia games". Each turn will decide between success or defeat for the next step.

The Oracle of Delphi, on the other hand, involved more uncertainties. The ambiguous prophecies were to be heeded with great caution as they often gave misleading assurances about the next step.

When the Persian emperor Darius was confronted with the decision of whether or not to wage war against Alexander the Great, he consulted the Oracle. Darius received the following answer to his question: "If you cross the Euphrates, you will destroy a great empire." Convinced of his victory, Darius proceeded with the battle against his enemy and suffered a crushing defeat. Indeed, he had destroyed a great empire – his own.

If you are able to understand Latin, you can instantly gather from the title of the following game ("I doubt") that you will be confronted with ambivalence about which decision to make during each step.

Dubito

Number of Players: 1 to 4
Length: 20 minutes
Components: 2 x 52 cards

Components: Two standard deck of 52 cards.

Game idea: One after the other, the players will play single cards in order to build a display of cards with four rows of (1) ascending, (2) same-suit, (3) same-suit ascending and finally (4) a row of cards of the same value.

Setup: After shuffling the decks deal each player a hand of eight cards. Place the remaining stack of cards face-down in the middle of the playing area and agree on which player begins.

Gameplay: The players take turns one after the other. When it is your turn, place one of your hand cards face-up into one of the four rows of your display. (In order to avoid any misconceptions, you should announce which row you are playing into during the first few turns.) To replenish your hand, draw a card from the stack, which ends your turn. Then, the next player will take their turn.

Display: During the course of the game, each player will create their own card display, which consists of four rows with any number of cards. The individual rows will be filled from left to right. The first card of each row can be any card, but all of the cards to come afterwards have to adhere to the following conditions:

Row 1 :	Each additional card must have a higher value than all preceding cards.
Row 2 :	All cards must have the same suit.
Row 3 :	All cards must have the same suit and, at the same time, each additional card must have a higher value than all preceding cards.
Row 4 :	All cards must have the same value.

The following is a typical example of such a display:

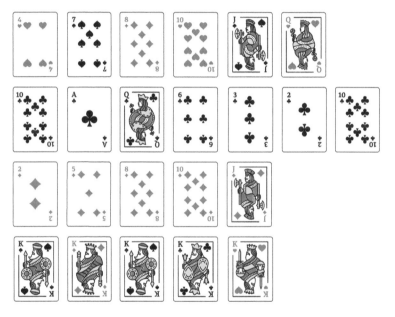

Game end: If a player is unable to play a card during their turn, their display is completed and the game is over for them. The other players continue the game, until they too reach their limits.

If you have completely depleted the card stack during the course of the game before finishing your displays (which will be the norm with four players), you can only play your remaining hand cards, after which the game is over. (If playing with a larger number of players, use three 52-card decks, so that you won't have to stop the game during the exciting end phase. The larger deck will actually allow some more interesting results.)

Scoring: After all players have finished their display, we can begin with the scoring:

For each card in the first row, you will receive a point, each card in the second row is worth two points, each card in the third row will net you three points and each card in the fourth row will get you four points.

For example, for the display pictured earlier, we would receive a total of 55 points. ($6 x 1 + 7 x 2 + 5 x 3 + 5 x 4 = 55$. If you take into account that four cards in a column are worth exactly ten points, you can calculate the value of your display much more easily: $5 x 10 + 1 x 1 + 2 x 2 = 55$.)

The player with the highest number of points in his display wins the game.

Game tactics: During the course of the game, you will have to make the right decisions at the right time. Which card value you collect in the fourth row of your display is your single most important decision here.

If you settle too early it is likely that you'll find that another choice would have been better. If you wait too long, however, you already might have put certain numbers into a less valuable row, which could lose a lot of possible points.

Of course, you might also have to make similar decisions for your third and second row. Generally speaking, you should pick two different suits here to be able to fit in as many of your hand cards as possible. In order to increase your options, it is also advisable to go with the numbers which you can't fit in anywhere else for the fourth row.

If you can manage to make a decision for a relatively valuable row towards the beginning (for example if you have three of the same number for the fourth row), then you are in an especially fortunate situation. You can start off by developing this row and win precious time this way, before you have to make more decisions.

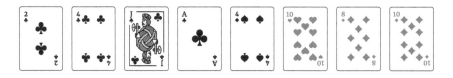

For example, the hand cards pictured above initially don't give you much indication as to what you should place in the fourth row. On the other hand, you can't really expect to get a stronger suit than Clubs any time soon. Consequently, you should first play the Two into the third row and the Four in the following round:

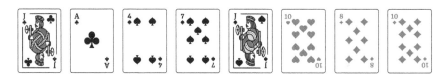

With the two new cards in our hand we now have a better idea what to base our next decisions on. For the third row, we will probably wait for a few more lower cards before playing the higher ones. After playing the Jack of Clubs there later on, we currently only really have the Ten for the fourth row. Considering this, we only have Spades left now as a second strong suit with which we can now continue our game in the second row.

As the different players don't affect each other directly, the one-player game of Dubito also offers you valuable experience. With multiple players, you should consider the cards your opponents use as well, though, and don't forget that the displays can also offer you some insight on the distribution of hand cards. Therefore, it might not be the best idea to use the same suits or even the same number as your opponents.

Variant: Subito

The mostly unwanted lack of cards towards the end of the game, which we mentioned earlier, can be used for a tactical variant when playing with three or four players. With only two players we can simply use just one regular deck of 52 cards. (For one player this variant does not really offer anything new when compared to the regular game.)

The game works the same way, except that you are now allowed to play multiple cards during each turn. After you have played all the cards you wanted to play, replenish your hand cards accordingly by drawing as many cards from the stack. This way, you have the chance to draw and play more cards than your opponents.

As you don't immediately replenish your hand after playing each card, you buy the higher number of cards by having less information, which brings additional risks.

Now, you should be particularly careful not to block your opportunities by playing too many cards at once. Otherwise, you will find yourself running out of options too early, and your opponents can use the remaining stack of cards for themselves. However, having a display full of possibilities when the stack is already depleted is as useless as having a finished display when a big stack still remains. Here more than ever, it is more about finding the right middle way between waiting and playing.

Variant: Judico

With two to four players, instead of giving eight cards to each player at the beginning of the game, you can put the whole stack of cards in the middle of the playing area and play without hand cards. During a one player game, you should only use one deck of 52 cards for this to make the game faster.

When it is your turn, reveal the top card of the stack and decide whether you want to play this card into your display or to discard it and put it into the discard pile. The cards in the discard pile are of no importance during the rest of the game and can be arranged face-up next to the stack.

As you can't keep the revealed cards anymore, you should relax the requirements for the rows to not make the game too dependent on luck. There are multiple possibilities for this:

If you still wish to play with four different rows, you should now build your display from two rows with red and two rows with black cards, with one red and one black row having ascending cards and the other two rows having descending cards.

The first card you play in a row will merely determine the color of the row, with only the second card defining whether you will need to play a higher or lower card afterwards.

It is up to you where to place each of these four rows within your display, it is only important that each type of row only occurs once.

In this variant, it is all about measuring the "bird in the hand" against the "two in the bush". Is it advisable to play the revealed card and make a few guaranteed points, or is it better to wait in order to maybe make more in the long run?

The following picture shows a typical display towards the end of the game:

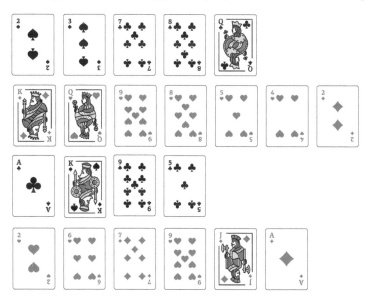

The game ends when all cards of the stack have been used or discarded. Each card in your display is then worth a point. Whoever has the most cards in their display wins the game.

Alternatively, you can also reduce the display in this variant to only have two rows, one with red ascending cards and the other with black ascending cards:

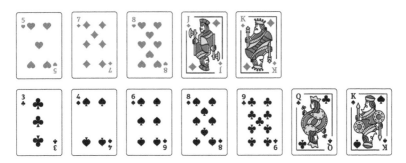

The game will become much more intense if there is only a single row with ascending cards (in any color):

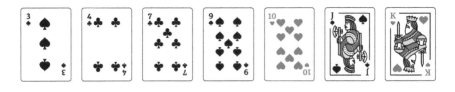

Suggestions

Do you know "Eleven Starts!" (*Elfer Raus*)? It is a popular card game based on a deck with 80 cards with the values from One to Twenty in four different colors. You can buy this card game cheaply in many stores and get a very versatile deck of cards, which you can use in many established games as an alternative to the usual 52 card deck.

Playing the games described in this book with this, or a similar deck of cards, offers some exciting variants with new tactical considerations.

SONO-GAMES

Tactics and luck are two decisive elements of many games. Chess and Roulette both serve here as extreme examples, which are found on opposite ends of the scale.

Often, the zest of good games is in the interactions of tactics and luck: without tactical opportunities to influence the game, we are at the mercy of chance. We can't contribute anything to our success and the luckiest player wins. On the other hand, games that are decided solely by the player's skills without any element of luck present us with a very different challenge. The more we plan ahead, the more success we will have. If we wanted to prepare properly, we possibly would never even make it past the first turn. Think about the gigantic scope of chess literature, for example.

A game which is defined by the tactics of the players, but still retains some element of luck frees us from taxing precalculations and still allows us to guide our approach. The better player wins. But no game is like any other, as there's always a variety of new situations in front of us to provide a challenge.

Sono

Number of Players: 2

Length: 15 minutes

Components: 52 cards, 1 Joker

Components: From a standard deck of 52 cards we will only use the cards from Nine to Ace (i.e. 9, 10, J, Q, K and A), and one Joker for a total of 25 cards.

Game idea: During the course of the game, the two players will create a five by five square made of cards together. One player will try to create the most valuable rows, the other will focus on the columns.

Setup: Shuffle the cards, give each player ten and place the remaining five cards face-down in a diagonal line of the square-to-be as shown in the illustration below. This also defines the locations of the rest of the cards. Agree with your opponent on who will play the five rows and who will play the columns of the square.

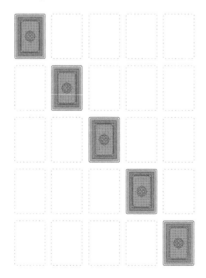

Gameplay: After you have dealt the cards, your opponent will begin with their turn. One after the other, your opponent and you will place a hand card face-up on a free spot of the emerging square. While doing so, each new card has to be adjacent to a card that has already been placed.

Any of the diagonally placed cards from the beginning will be revealed when it has at least two adjacent cards. This way, the information from those cards will slowly enter the game as it progresses. You can find an example for this below:.

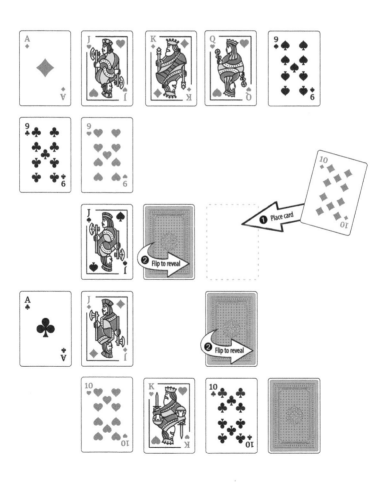

As soon as the last of the diagonal cards has been revealed, you and your opponent should also reveal the rest of your hand cards and continue with open hands. (The opponent's hand could now be calculated anyway, this way you can save yourself the trouble and the game will continue more swiftly.) When all hand cards have been played, the square is completed and the game is over.

Scoring: The scores for the five rows and the five columns of the square will be calculated according to the following list. While doing so, you and your opponent, independently from each other, can use the joker in one of their own lines as any card, so the score will be as high as possible.

Pair (two of the same value)   1 point

Two Pairs   2 points

Triplets (three of the same value)   3 points

Full House (Triplets awnd Pair) 5 points

Straight (five sequential cards) 5 points

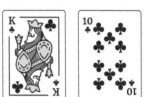   

Quadruplets (four of the same value) 6 points

Quintuplets (five of the same value) 10 points

Clan (five red or five black cards, five spot cards (Nines, Tens, Aces) or five face cards (Jacks, Queens, Kings)) 3 points

The categories from Pair to Quintuplets are mutually exclusive, but Clans are scored in addition to any other category present in a line. Quintuplets in particular will also always cause a Clan (five spot or five face cards). For the following card combination, you can get a total of 11 points with the Joker as a Ten of Spades (Full House and two Clans, one with black cards and another with spot cards):

Game Tactics: Play quickly! There's more to learn from multiple short games and they are also more fun than a never-ending game in which you try to play perfectly.

At the beginning, you should briefly analyze your hand cards. Do you have three or even four cards with the same value and therefore good prospects for a high score? What could be your opponent's strengths?

The central card combination in Sono is the Triplets. They can be created relatively easily, despite any effort of your opponent and they also provide a reasonable amount of points. All higher combinations can be prevented fairly easily with the right moves: Full House, Straight, Quintuplets, and Clans can be averted easily by placing a mismatched card in the corresponding line. Keep in mind that the existence of both a Nine and an Ace is the only possibility of destroying a Straight without causing a Pair. In order to prevent Quadruplets you will have to play a mismatched third card to an already existing Pair. Whenever a line has Triplets it will already have at least four cards, and you will reach your goal with a mismatched fifth card. Interfere with your opponent every chance that you get!

Of course, when actually playing the game it sometimes is not that easy. Firstly, you can't influence the diagonal cards, and secondly you don't always have the right card to block your opponent – especially towards the end of the game. Balancing your hand cards is important to prevent opposing card combinations as well as developing your own. And then there's still the Joker, whose timing and placement in the square is particularly important. Therefore, use your chances!

With each card you play, you should try improving your own lines as well as destroying your opponent's. In the same process, try to pay special attention to potential Clans.

Variant: Strategic Sono

In contrast to the regular game, you can agree with your opponent that new cards in the square have to be placed so that they are adjacent to at least two other cards.

This reduces the number of possible placements for your hand cards, which has the consequence of not having all lines directly available any longer. Thus, a back and forth for the most interesting spaces in the square, which now have to be enabled by prior placements, begins. In addition to the struggle for the most valuable card combinations, there are now also fights for strategic positions.

Variant: Open Sono

At the beginning of the game, reveal the ten cards of each player and also place the remaining five cards face-up when creating the diagonal line with them. Then, continue as you would in the regular game.

This is a variant which emphasizes analytical thinking as well as planning ahead and may also end up taking longer. - For people who are fond of mental exercises this might be a more fitting alternative.

As a shorter variant, you can place the five diagonal cards face-up at the beginning and form a face-down stack with the rest of the cards. Taking turns, your opponent and you will then draw a card and place it as in the regular game until the stack is depleted and the square has been filled. The scoring will take place as before.

Tactics-wise, you will have fewer will opportunities in this variant. Now, you can only decide the placement of your card, but not which card to place. But you can now take higher risks, as your opponent also has to wait for the right chance to complete their combination. Here, it is all about weighing your risks and chances against each other, as luck will play an important role too.

A modification of the two Open Sono variants is created when scoring after each new card, though it also requires more writing: whoever increases the score of a line or even two with their card placement receives the corresponding number of points of these lines. (Alternatively, you can also only count the increase of the score rather than the score of the whole line.) You can pick a new card for the Joker each time a line with it is scored.

For example, you would receive 3 points for the situation depicted below. (The value of the row improves from a Pair to Triplets, the column stays the same and therefore won't be added.)

Generally speaking, you should try to place the last card of the individual lines, as you have the best chances here to increase your score as well as creating the highest scoring patterns.

Variant: Cooperative Sono

You can also agree with your partner to cooperate and try to achieve the highest possible score of all rows and columns without changing the game play rules of the regular game.

This will bring about new tactical considerations, which we will examine further in the following one player Unisono.

Suggestions

By changing the 25 card deck the game is based on, you will find entirely new aspects: if you create your own cards with the values from One to Five in five different colors, the game will obtain a particularly nice symmetry.

Coming up with the most interesting ways of scoring will be a challenge for your creativity. For example, turn your attention to especially high or low sums of the five values in a line, and award more points the farther the sum is from the average value of 15. Or you could make it a challenge to create as many variants for this new deck as possible.

Maybe you will also have fun playing Sono with a bigger or smaller card square. Modify your deck to account for the different number of cards and create new scoring rules.

Unisono

Number of Players: 1
Length: 10 minutes
Components: 52 cards, 1 Joker

Components: We will use the same 25 card deck as in Sono, meaning the cards from Nine to Ace (i.e. 9, 10, J, Q, K and A), and one Joker.

Game idea: Unisono is the one player game of the Sono family: the goal is to create a five by five square of cards with the highest possible value in the rows and columns.

Setup: Shuffle the cards, then place the top five cards face-down as the diagonal of the square-to-be from the top left to the bottom right, just like in Sono. Keep the other 20 cards as a face-down stack.

Gameplay: One at a time, draw a card and place that card face-up into a free space of the square, adjacent to at least one already existing card.

If, during the course of the game, one of the diagonal cards is adjacent to at least two other cards, reveal that card. When all diagonal cards have been revealed and each free spot in the square is adjacent to at least one card, you can reveal the card stack and continue playing that way. (The remaining cards could be calculated any way and the order doesn't matter any longer.) When the whole square has been filled, the game ends.

Scoring: Scoring is the same as in Sono, though now the sum of rows and columns both will count for you.

Game tactics: To improve the information you have at your disposal, you should try to reveal the diagonal cards as quickly as possible. Afterwards, you should make all spaces available in order to continue with open cards.

You will have fewer conflicts between the rows and columns if you focus on Straights and Clans of the same color in the columns and try for multiples of the same value and Clans from face or spot cards in the rows.

Variant: Open Unisono

If you like puzzle games, you can also play with the diagonal line revealed from the start, taking the other 20 cards as hand cards and then, with all information available, think about how to create the most valuable square.

Question 11

Maximum Unisono: How many points can you possibly score (with optimal placement of the diagonal)?

? Question 12

Minimum Unisono: What is the lowest possible score, when you can choose the diagonal again and the Joker accordingly as well? How does the score change if the Joker has to be chosen so that it increases the scores of the affected lines as much as possible?

Quasono

Number of Players: 4
Length: 15 minutes
Components: 52 cards, 1 Joker

Components: Once again, we will use the same 25 cards as with Sono, meaning the cards from Nine to Ace (i.e. 9, 10, J, Q, K and A), and one Joker.

Game idea: Quasono is the four player team game of the Sono family: two players each will form a team. During the course of the game, all four players together will create a five by five square of cards. One team will try to create the most valuable rows, the other will focus on the columns.

Setup: Shuffle the cards, give each player five of them, and place the remaining five cards face-up as a diagonal of the square-to-be from the top left to the bottom right, just like in Sono.

Players sitting opposite from each other will form a team and will play together. Agree on which team will play for the rows and which for the columns.

Gameplay: After all players have received their five hand cards, each player chooses two of them and hands them face-down to their partner. The received cards can be looked at and placed into their hand only after cards have already been given. Aside from this initial exchange of information no more communication between partners is allowed.

Starting with the player sitting to the left of the dealer, the players will take turns placing one of their hand cards face-up into one of the free spots of the square, which has to be adjacent to at least one already existing card. When all hand cards have been played, the square is finished and the game is over.

Scoring: The scoring is the same as in Sono. The team which was able to achieve a higher score with their five lines wins the game.

Game tactics: Generally speaking, the same considerations as in Sono also apply here. However, by forming teams there are some additional aspects. The exchange of cards at the beginning is the only means of communication within the team. If the Joker is among your hand cards, you should give it to your partner. This way, you will make it clear that this most important card is in your team rather than your opponent's. If you have multiple cards with the same value, it is recommended to give one of them to your partner to be able to place the right card combinations quickly during the course of the game.

As you only have a few hand cards, it is important to use the card swap to have a balanced hand, containing red and black as well as face and spot cards in roughly equal numbers.

It is self-evident that you should memorize the cards you gave to your partner as well as the ones you received and be aware of them throughout the course of the game. After all, with that information you already know nearly half of their hand. If you also only play the exchanged cards towards the end of the game, you will have a better idea of the whole card distribution. Especially during the final stages of the game, you should be aware of which cards you can still expect from your partner as well as your opponents.

Variant: Double Quasono

In contrast to the regular game you can form teams from the players sitting next to each other, who will take their turns after each other.

As an additional rule, you could also introduce the second player of a team having to play into the same row or column as their partner – if possible.

This has interesting consequences. The game will now progress in individual waves, with the first player of each team taking some sort of leadership role.

Suggestions

After Sono, Unisono, and Quasono we're only missing a real Sono variant for three players: Trisono.

With our previous card square we would have some difficulties, as we need lines in three different directions. But maybe you could try experimenting with a card triangle, for example in the following shape:

EXCURSION INTO PROBABILITY CALCULATION

Do you know the tale of the poor prisoner, who is told the following: "You will be executed next week. The day of the execution between Monday and Friday will be a complete surprise."

Full of despair, the prisoner remains in his cell. But suddenly, he starts thinking: "The execution next week can't be a surprise! If I still live on Thursday evening, the execution on Friday wouldn't really be much of a surprise anymore. Consequently, it can't be Friday and the last possible date of the execution is Thursday. However, if I still live on Wednesday evening, then the execution on Thursday won't be much of a surprise, so that it can't be this day as well, meaning Wednesday can be the last possible date for the execution. But similarly, it also can't be Wednesday, Tuesday or even Monday, meaning that the execution is not at all possible!"

To his complete surprise, the prisoner is executed on the Tuesday of the following week.

In order to be spared similar surprises, we want to examine the probabilities of uncertain events in this chapter. Once again this will involve a bit of number crunching.

Excursion into Probability Calculation

Probability calculation is all about random processes where different events can happen. The aim of probability calculation is to determine the likelihood that specific events will occur. We will do a bit of mathematics to figure out the frequency of various outcomes which are determined by luck.

Elementary events: Here, we will initially only look at random processes which are based on a fixed number of events and are all mutually exclusive. During the course of one such process exactly one of the possible events can occur.

If there is no reason to assume that individual events will occur more often than others, we will say these events are "equally likely".

For example, when rolling a symmetrical die, we can assume that on average, none of the six sides will be rolled more often than any other. Therefore, this is a random process with the six equally likely elementary events from One to Six. (In reality, each die may have slight asymmetries, which we will disregard here.)

Whenever a random process is based on a number of exactly n different elementary events, we define the number 1/n as the probability of the occurrence of such an event. (n here refers to any natural number 1, 2, 3 ...)

For example, the probability for the appearance of each of the six sides on a symmetrical die is 1/6. Rolling two (differently colored) dice can have one of the following 36 different outcomes where each number in a pair represents one die:

11	21	31	41	51	61
12	22	32	42	52	62
13	23	33	43	53	63
14	24	34	44	54	64
15	25	35	45	55	65
16	26	36	46	56	66

Apparently, there is also no reason here why, when using symmetrical dice, all of the results shouldn't be equally likely. The probability of each of these elementary events is therefore 1/36.

If we draw a card from a shuffled deck of 52 cards, the probability for drawing a certain card is 1/52. In a card deck with 32 cards, the probability is 1/32.

In a horse race, the individual horses are usually not exactly equally strong. Therefore, the assumption that the probability that each horse may win is equally likely is not correct. The same thing is true for the outcome of a soccer game.

Composite events: The effects of randomness or chance is not limited to single or elementary events, but can also affect the outcome of composite events which are made up of a number of elementary outcomes.

Examples for such composite events might include rolling an even number with a die since this can happen if any one of three elementary events occur — namely rolling a Two or Four or Six. Similarly drawing a Queen from a deck of cards has happened if any one of four elementary events occurs (Queen of Hearts or Queen of Clubs or Queen of Diamonds or Queen of Spades).

When a composite event consists of k possibilities from a total of n different elementary events, we define the probability for this event by adding the individual probabilities as k/n. (k is a natural number here which can't be greater than n.) Impossible events, in which none of the elementary events would be a success, have a probability of 0.

For example, an even number occurs with a probability of 3/6 = 1/2 when rolling a die. A number of seven or more cannot be rolled with the role of a single die, so that this event will be assigned a probability of 0/6 = 0. However, the probability of getting any number between One and Six is 6/6 = 1.

The probability of drawing a Queen (any Queen) from a deck of 52 cards is 4/52 = 1/13. A Heart card (any Hearts card) is drawn with a probability of 13/52 = 1/4

In order to roll a total sum of four when using two (differently colored) dice, one of the elementary events 13 (that is the dice faces read 1 & 3), 22, or 31 has to occur. Consequently, this composite event has a probability of 3/36 = 1/12.

 Question 13

Probability of total value II: When rolling two dice, the result can be any number from two to twelve. Determine the probability of each possible sum.

Law of large numbers: Each event has a probability that is between 0 and 1. The probability of 0 indicates an impossible event. An event with a probability of 1 means that it will always occur.

If we test the outcome of a particular random process multiple times, the different probabilities offer us a measure for the frequency the individual events will occur:

For example, when rolling a die, a Two will appear roughly every sixth roll. Therefore, we also say that the event is to be expected in 1/6 or 16.7% of all cases.

This is only a statistical statement, from which a practical, individual case can more or less deviate simply because chance is involved. Mathematics does offer us a reassuring estimate, however:

Law of large numbers: Even the smallest deviation from the percentage given by the probabilities becomes less and less likely the more times this random process is repeated.

 Question 14

Distribution of winnings: Two players flip a coin. Whenever the coin lands on heads, one of the players gets a point, whereas the other gets a point whenever it lands on tails. The agreement is that the player who has five points first wins the game and gets the wager. Due to unforeseen circumstances the game is cut short with a score of 4:3. The players don't feel that, dividing the bet at a rate of 4:3 (points scored) or at 2:1 (points missing for the win) is fair. How should the bet be split among the two players when it is to be divided based on their chance of winning the game?

The law of large numbers can also be used to experimentally approximate probabilities of asymmetric processes (for example of a loaded die).

For example, suppose we toss a thumbtack 1000 times (or toss 1000 identical tacks) and tally the position that each tack lands in. If it lands on its head 406 times and ends up lying on its side (rim and pointed tip) 594 times we can estimate the probability of it landing on its head at roughly 406/1000 or roughly 2/5.

Examples of combinatorics: Our definition of probabilities "only" requires that we count the outcome of individual cases and divide them by the total number of elementary events (after determining all elementary events it is based on). In more complex situations, the counting methods we discussed in the previous excursion into combinatorics will come in quite handy. Utilizing what we have learned there will lead us to the following conclusions:

Four dice can have a total of 1296 different results (elementary events). 360 of these consist of four different numbers. The likelihood of having four different numbers when rolling four dice is therefore 360/1296 = 5/18 or roughly 28%. Conversely, about 72% of all rolls contain at least two of the same number.

In order to guarantee the equiprobability of our elementary events, we will have to assume the combinatorial distinguishability of the individual dice (for example each might be a different color), even if we subjectively don't pay any attention to it.

When rolling three Ones and one Two, it certainly does matter which die resulted in a Two. There are four different possibilities for this, whereas there is only really one way four Ones can occur. Three Ones and one Two (with a sum of 5) therefore occur with a probability of 4/1296 = 1/324, or four times as often as four Ones (with a sum of 4), which has a probability of only 1/1296.

....

 Question 15

....

Coin toss II: What is the probability of flipping ten coins resulting in exactly five heads and five tails? What is the probability of having at least six heads?

In the 649 lotteries (based on selecting 6 numbers from 49), there are a total of 13983816 different tickets. Only one of them will match all six drawn numbers, so that the probability for that happening is roughly 1 to 14 million. The following table uses the results of our excursion into combinatorics and tells us the likelihood of all winning groups:

Number of matches	Probability
6	1/13983816 = 0.000007%
5	258/13983816 = 0.0018%
4	13545/13983816 = 0.09%
3	246820/13983816 = 1.8%

The probability of winning anything is therefore around 1.9%, meaning that over 98% of all tickets win nothing at all. (We will disregard the complementary bonus or "extra" number present in some lotteries. The probability for the category "Five matches + bonus number" is 6/13983816 = 0.00004%.)

 Question 16

Poker II: What is the probability of a player receiving the following five card hands when playing poker with 32 cards?

1. five different card values
2. at least one Pair (two of the same value)
3. Three of a Kind (three of the same value) and Four of a Kind
4. a Flush (five cards of the same suit), a Straight (five cards in sequence), a Royal Flush (five cards in sequence of the same suit)

Multiplication principle: Multiple random processes are independent from each other when each individual process is not affected by the results of the other processes. If we roll a die twice, the result of one roll is independent from the second. No matter which number is the result, all six numbers in the second roll have the same probability of 1/6.

The probability of multiple random processes having certain results independently from each other can be calculated as the product of the individual probabilities. Let's look at the example of rolling a die and the probability of rolling a Two followed by an even number. Probability of rolling a Two is 1/6. Probability of rolling an even number is ½. So, the probability of rolling a Two followed by an even number afterwards is 1/6 x 1/2 = 1/12. (That is also the same probability of rolling an even number followed by a Two!)

However, if we draw two cards consecutively (without putting any back) from a deck of 52 cards, these random processes are not independent from each other. The card which was drawn first has a probability of 0 when drawing the second card, whereas all other cards have a probability of 1/51. Depending on which card appears first, the probabilities change with the second drawing. (If the first card was put into the stack immediately after drawing it, the two drawings would be independent from each other.)

A typical application of the multiplication principle is the problem of calculating the appearance of at least one occurrence of a certain result within multiple tries. The easiest method is to calculate the probability of the result not occurring at all, in order to calculate the probability we are looking for. Based on that:

Alex and Claus are shooting at a target at the same time. Alex hits with a probability of 3/4 and Claus with a probability of 2/3. What is the probability of the target being hit at least once?

Obviously, the probability of Alex missing the target is 1-3/4 = 1/4 and with Claus 1- 2/3 = 1/3. As the shots are independent of each other, the two shooters will miss the target at the same time with a probability of 1/4 x 1/3 = 1/12. As a result, the probability of the target being hit at least once is   1-1/12 = 11/12, or roughly 88%.

After both shots have been made, if we can recognize that the target has been hit exactly once, how big is the likelihood of the shot being from Claus?

The probability of Alex hitting the target and Claus missing turns out to be 3/4 x 1/3 = 3/12. For Alex missing and Claus hitting at the same time, the probability is 1/4 x 2/3 = 2/12. As these are the only two possibilities of hitting the target exactly once, we can see that in 60% of the cases Alex will be the one to hit the target and Claus during the other 40%.

Is it possible to set up a shooting schedule where Alex can occasionally hit the target with an accuracy of at least 99%?

With three shots, the probability of missing every time is still above 1% with 1/4 x 1/4 x 1/4 = 1/64, although with four shots it drops to 1/4 x 1/4 x 1/4 x 1/4 = 1/256 so that the probability of success is now clearly above 99%.

 ## Question 17

Birthday problem: Suppose that you have a room containing 23 people. What is the probability that at least two people in the room have the same birthday? Begin with an intuitive guess and then let yourself be surprised by the calculated result. (Assume that each of the 365 days is equally likely as the birthday of a person, and start by calculating the probability of the birthdays of all 23 people being on different days.)

Expected value: It is often interesting to know the average result of a random process. Here, we are only talking about random processes which only have numerical results, or we can assign meaningful numerical values to the different events. To determine the average value, we multiply all possible results with their corresponding probability of occurrence and then add all resulting products together. The sum calculated this way is also referred to as expected value of the random process it is based on.

For example, the expected value of rolling a die is 1/6 x 1 + 1/6 x 2 + 1/6 x 3 + 1/6 x 4 + 1/6 x 5 + 1/6 x 6 = 3.5.

Flipping three coins can have the following eight results when considering all possible combinations of heads (H) and tails (T): HHH, HHT, HTH, THH, HTT, THT, TTH, TTT. If we are only interested in the number of heads, we will have an expected value of $1/8x0 + 3/8x1 + 3/8x2 + 1/8x3 = 1.5$.

In Roulette, you can bet a coin on one of the 37 numbers from 0 to 36. If you have the winning number, you win 35 coins. $(1/37 \times 35)$ Otherwise, you lose your bet. $(36/37 \times (-1))$ This gives us an expected value of $1/37 \times 35 + 36/37 \times (-1) = -1/37$.

Of course, the expected value of a random process is only a statistically informative value, and the actual outcome of an individual case can deviate from this substantially. As a consequence of the law of large numbers, however, we will realize that even small deviations between the average and expected value become more and more unlikely when increasing the number of repetitions. The expected value therefore gives us information about which result we can expect long-term with any given random process.

If the expected value of a random process is negative, there is a high probability that we will have losses over multiple repetitions, whereas with a positive expected value we can at least count on a positive outcome long-term. The expected value 0 represents a fair random process in which we neither have an advantage nor a disadvantage.

After these considerations, it is clear why we have a negative expected value when playing Roulette. On average, the bank wins 1/37 or about 3% of all bets. (All payouts are devised in such a way that Roulette with the numbers of 1 to 36 would be a fair game. The additional number 0 represents the profit margin of the casino.)

? Question 18

Lottery: To enter a lottery, you pay $10 and choose a number between One and Six. Afterwards, two dice are rolled. If your number is rolled, you win $30, otherwise you get nothing. Calculate the expected value of this lottery. How much would the price of the lottery have to be in order to have a fair game?

In many cases, the expected value gives us a reasonable basis for evaluating a random process. However, sometimes the excitement of a game or hoping for good luck causes us to accept even unfavorable random processes. This is the business of gambling houses, and Roulette is an example of this. (Small bets with the prospect of high winnings.)

On the other hand, we might also pass on favorable random processes in extreme situations, if a negative outcome could mean our downfall, for example. This is why insurance companies are so successful. Compared to the expected value of a claim, premiums put us in a worse position as a result of the administrative costs in relationship to the acceptance of risks. (Small bets with the prospect of preventing high losses.)

DECATHLON

Decathletes are regarded as the exemplification of athletes. Running, jumping, and throwing are all on the menu. That means that the entirety of the athlete's physical abilities are required.

At the same time, a decathlon is more than just a sequence of ten individual, energy-sapping disciplines. The constant change of movements and continual adjustment towards the next peak performance requires a high amount of concentration. Processing the intermediate results along the way and the continuous confrontation with the opponents creates enormous pressures.

It is all about knowing your risks and chances, and rationing your energy reserves to reach the limits of your capabilities.

The following game is a simple simulation of a decathlon, in which your success mostly depends on your tactical abilities.

Decathlon

Number of Players: 1 to 4
Length: 15 minutes per player
Components: 8 dice, score sheet

Components: We need the score sheet below, which you should copy, and 8 dice.

Game idea: The game takes place over ten events, in which the players will battle in different ways for as many points as possible. At the end, the player with the highest total score wins.

Setup: Assign a column to each player on the score sheet by writing their name into the first row. Also, determine the order in which you will complete the first event.

Gameplay: Play the individual events of the decathlon one after the other in the order indicated on the score sheet. Starting with the second event, the player in the lead will always roll first and the better players will take their turns before the lower scoring ones. (In case of a tie determine the player who goes first randomly; if the players have vastly different amounts of experience, you can also agree on having more experienced players go first.)

If an event takes place over multiple tries, all players should complete their first try before you continue with the additional attempts. The player order will stay the same during all attempts.

Only during the high jump and pole vault should players each complete their three attempts per height in a row, for clarity's sake. The jump height will only be adjusted after all players had their turn. You will only have to decide if you want to attempt any given height or not when it is your turn.

Decathlon				
100 meters				
Long jump				
Shot put				
High jump				
400 meters				
110 m hurdles				
Discus throw				
Pole Vault				
Javelin throw				
1500 meters				

Record your individual results immediately on the score sheet after each turn. Use the boxes on the left in your column for this.

Then, add the best result of each player to their score after each event. This will give you the current standings and the player order for the next event. Record the new score in the right box in the current column.

As the different events are independent from each other, you can start the game after reading the rules to the first event:

100 meters: 8 dice, 1 attempt   up to 40 points

Start by rolling four dice. If you are not satisfied with your roll, you have the opportunity to re-roll them multiple times. After you are done with the first roll, roll the other four dice, which you can also re-roll multiple times. In total, you can only re-roll dice a total of five times, so that you reach the goal after seven rolls, at most.

Your result is the sum of all eight dice, however, any sixes are counted negatively and are deducted from your result.

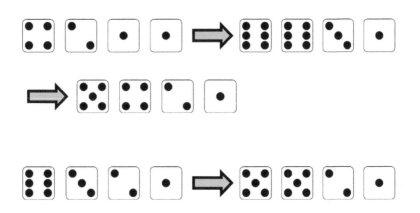

In the run pictured above, you would get a total of 25 points after the three re-rolls (indicated by the arrows) (5 + 4 + 2 + 1 + 5 + 5 + 2 + 1 = 25).

In a track meet, a long jump consists of the "approach run" and the actual jump. Starting with five dice, you can roll the dice multiple times during the approach phase. The goal is to have as many dice as possible while keeping the total sum at nine or under. You must keep at least one die after each roll, so that this phase is completed after the fifth roll, if not before. Once a die has been kept once cannot be re-rolled again during the approach phase.

Here, you should try to roll as low as possible, because as soon as the sum of the kept dice is over nine, you have crossed the foul line. That means your attempt is invalid and will be scored as 0 points.

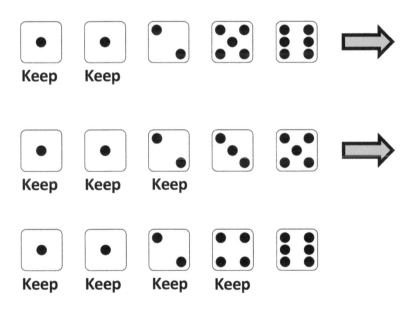

Generally speaking, you should end the run-up phase in the situation above $(1 + 1 + 2 + 4 = 8)$, as you would have to roll a one to not cross the foul line if you re-rolled again.

As long as the sum of the kept dice is no higher than nine, you can move on to the jump phase at any time. For this, you will only use the dice you kept. (The other dice won't be used.) Take these dice and roll them. You can roll them multiple times, although you will have to keep an additional die after each roll again.

This time, your goal is the high numbers, as the score of your jump will be the sum of these dice.

The following jump with four dice would net you 18 points, for example (6 + 6+ 5 + 1 = 18):

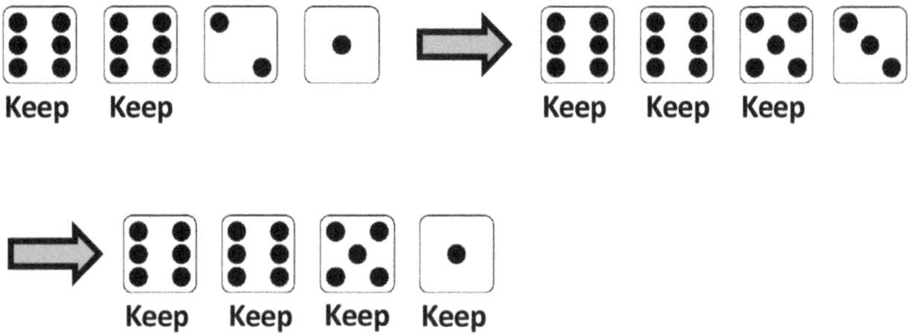

Shot put: 8 dice, 3 attempts up to 40 points

Roll up to eight dice individually, one after the other. If a Six is rolled, you have crossed the circle. Your attempt is then invalid and will be scored with 0 points.

As long as no Six has been rolled, you can end your put at any time and record the sum of all rolled dice on the score sheet as the result of your attempt.

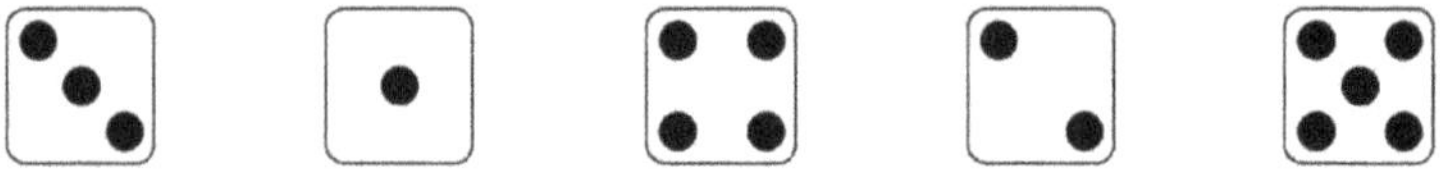

For example, you could end your first attempt with the shot put worth 15 points above $(3 + 1 + 4 + 2 + 5 = 15)$ and hope for a better result during the next attempts.

High jump: 5 dice, 3 attempts per height   up to 30 points

The jump heights of 10, 12, 14, 16 and so on will be announced in sequence. Each time, you can decide whether to skip the height or to attempt the jump. If you jump, you will have three attempts each time to make that jump.

To execute your jump, simply roll five dice. If the sum of the dice is at least as high as the announced height, you have successfully made that jump.

If you have three unsuccessful attempts in any height, the high jump is over for you. As a result, you will receive the score of the highest height you mastered. If you don't have a single valid attempt, you will get 0 points.

If you, for example, skip the heights of 10 and 12 and jump at 14, you would be successful during your second attempt in the following situation $(6 + 6 + 5 + 2 + 1 = 20)$:

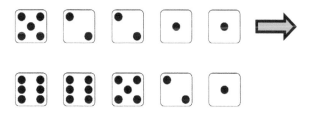

If you also skip height 16 and then fail all three attempts at height 18, you would end up with the 14 points for the highest jump that you successfully cleared.

400 meters: 8 dice, 1 attempt,   up to 40 points

Use four pairs with two dice each. Roll each pair one after the other, and after each roll you have the opportunity to roll that pair again, multiple times. Only when a pair is kept, continue to the next one. In total, you can only re-roll dice a total of five times, so that you reach the goal after a maximum of nine rolls, at most.

As a result, you will receive the sum of all eight dice as your score. However, any Sixes are counted negatively and are deducted from your score.

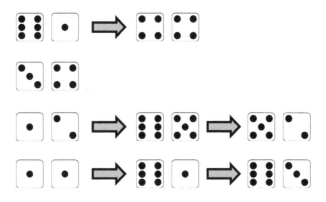

The run pictured above, utilizing all five re-rolls, would score a total of 19 points (4 + 4 + 3 + 4 + 5 + 2 − 6 + 3 = 19).

110 meter hurdles: 5 dice, 1 attempt   up to 30 points

Roll five dice. If you don't like the roll, you can re-roll it up to five times. So, you will reach the goal after the sixth roll, at most.

Your score is the sum of your last roll.

In the following example, you would receive 21 points after the second roll (6 + 6 + 5 + 3 + 1 = 21):

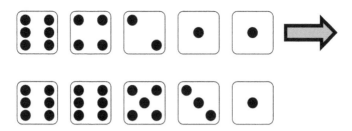

Discus throw: 5 dice, 3 attempts
up to 30 points

Starting with five dice, you can roll them multiple times. You must keep at least one die after each roll and any dice that are kept must show an even number. This phase is completed after the fifth roll, if not before..

If you roll exclusively odd numbers and therefore can't satisfy the requirements, you have crossed the circle. Your attempt is then invalid and worth 0 points.

As long as your attempt is still valid, you can end your throw at any time and record the sum of the kept dice as your score on the score sheet.

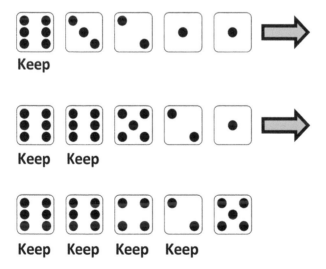

In the example above you could try to re-roll the last die and hope to get another even number for an even higher score. However, the risk of rolling an odd number and consequently losing the whole roll is rather big…50%! If you don't have a high result yet, it would be advisable to keep the roll in this situation and end it with 18 points (6 + 6 + 4 + 2 = 18).

Pole vault: 8 dice, 3 attempts per height   up to 40 points

The jump heights of 10, 12, 14, 16 and so on will be announced in sequence. As with the high jump, you can decide for each height whether you want to skip it or to attempt the jump. If you jump, you will have three attempts each time to successfully make the jump.

To execute your attempt, roll between one and eight dice. If the roll does not contain any Sixes and the sum is at least as high as the announced height, the jump is successful. Otherwise, the attempt is invalid. (Before each roll, you may choose the number of dice again.)

If you have three invalid attempts when trying to reach a height, pole vaulting is over for you. As a result, you will receive the highest successful jump's height as score.

If you don't even have a single successful jump, you will get no points for this event.

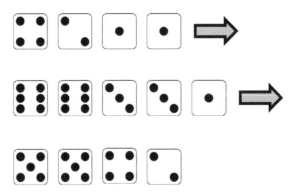

For example, in the situation above you would have only successfully jumped a height of 10 during the third attempt (5 + 5 + 4 + 2 = 16). If we also skip the heights of 12 and 14 and fail all three attempts of 16, we would only receive 10 points for this event.

Javelin throw: 6 dice, 3 attempts
up to 30 points

Starting with six dice, you can roll the dice multiple times, though once again you have to keep at least one die with each roll. In contrast to the discus throw, all kept dice must have an odd number.

If a roll only contains even numbers and therefore doesn't meet the requirements, you have crossed the line. Your attempt is then invalid and will be scored with 0 points.

As long as your attempt is still valid, you can end your throw at any time, scoring the sum of all odd dice.

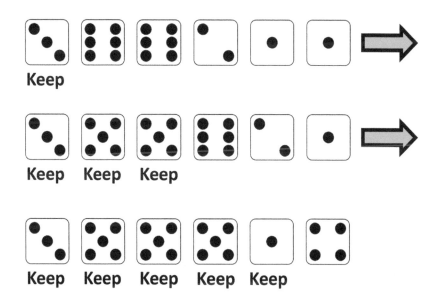

If you decided to end this current attempt, you score 19 points (3 + 5 + 5 + 5 + 1 = 19).

1500 meters: 8 dice, 1 attempt up to 40 points

Roll the dice individually, one after the other. After each roll, you have the option of re-rolling that die. Only after you have decided to keep a die can you roll the next one. With all eight dice you are only allowed five re-rolls in total, so that after 13 rolls at most you will have reached your goal.

The sum of all eight dice in this last event will be recorded as your score. The Sixes once again are counted negatively and are subtracted from your score.

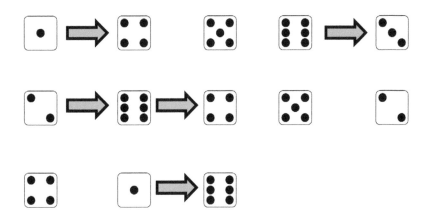

In the run pictured above, you would score 21 points (4 + 5 + 3 + 4 + 5 + 2 + 4 – 6 = 21).

Game end: When all ten events have been played, the game is over. It is possible to earn a score of up to 350 points. The player with the most points wins the game.

Game tactics: As the individual events are independent from each other, we can analyze each event on its own:

In the running events, you can score the highest amount of points. It's all about developing a feeling for when to re-roll the dice. If you risk too much and lose your strength too early, you might not have much luck towards the end. If you are too careful and keep low rolls, however, you are wasting your potential.

Question 19

Runs without Sixes: During the 100 meters you will roll four dice up to seven times, during the 400 meters two dice up to nine times, and during the 1500 meters one die up to 13 times. How many rolls without Sixes can you expect during each run? (Start by thinking about what percentage of the rolls contain no Sixes.) What conclusions can you draw from your result for re-rolling dice?

With all other events, you usually have multiple attempts. It is often a good idea to start by having a safe score and then use your other attempts to take higher risks and try for a higher score. This is especially important with the shot put, discus, and javelin throw events.

Question 20

Shot put: What is the percentage likelihood of a shot still being valid after the first, second, third etc. to the eighth roll? How many points will the shot contain on average? How many points might you lose on average if you continue your attempt? (Keep in mind that each valid die will bring you three points on average, and having an invalid roll will cause you to lose all points.)

With the jumping events, the pole vault will probably cause you the most problems. As each decision to jump contains a new risk, you should only jump a certain number of heights, just as with the high jump. Furthermore, you have to choose the number of dice in such a way so that you will have enough to make the jump, but also limit the risk of rolling a Six. The following question focusses on this problem:

Pole vault: With how many dice do you have the best chances of jumping the first height successfully? What is the expected percentage that you will fail all three times on the first height?

As the players have no direct influence on each other, you can gather some experience during a one player game. However, you should keep in mind that in a multiplayer game, a player who is behind may have to take higher risks in order to still have a chance at turning the tide. This way, the current rankings certainly will influence your decision-making process.

Variant: Decathlon with Energy

Decathlon can be significantly expanded by assigning each player a certain amount of energy at the beginning. Depending on how restrictive you want the game to be, you should assign 50, 60, or 70 energy units. For this variant, we need an extended score sheet, in which the individual energy units are represented as boxes. This will be at the top of the sheet above the 100 meter race scoring boxes:

Decathlon				
Energy Remaining				
100 meter				

During the whole contest, each roll (no matter with how many dice) uses up one unit of energy, which you have to cross out on the score sheet.

With this, you should make the following modifications to the regular game: during the shot put, you can now not only roll each die individually, but also roll any number of dice at the same time. During all four running events, you can re-roll the last roll as many times as you wish. If your energy reserves are all used up, you cannot roll any dice anymore, ending the game for you.

As the number of energy units is very limited, you will need a lot of experience to know where to use your energy units best. Generally speaking, you won't be able to get close to the maximum amount of points in the various events anymore, so now it is more about getting an acceptable result with the fewest number of rolls. Abort your least promising attempts during the jumping and throwing events early to preserve energy. Especially try to keep your number of attempts as low as possible and pass on additional attempts if you already have a good result. Also keep in mind that the 400 meters and the 1500 meters are very energy-sapping and therefore don't burn yourself out too early.

As an additional scoring variant, you may choose to add any remaining energy units to your final score. For example, if you complete the game that started with seventy energy units and still have 9 units left at the end of the game, 9 points would be added to your final score.

Variant: Duelathlon

With two or more players you can also assign points to the players depending on the rankings in the individual events. Each event will now be decided by an immediate head-to-head struggle.

At the end of each event, the player with the best result gets as many points as there are players. The next player gets a point less than that and so on, with the last player only receiving a single point.

Ties are broken by player order, with the player who started earliest in a particular event getting the better rank. Therefore, later players can adjust their play style depending on the result of earlier players, but they are disadvantaged during ties.

If a player does not even have a valid result to show for their turn, they are not able to be ranked and will receive no points.

Tactics-wise, you will have to pay attention to the results of your opponents. It is not about having the highest sum, but only leaving as many opponents behind as possible.

With energy reserves, Duelathlon will become particularly thrilling.

Suggestions

Of course, you can also modify individual events or add new ones to change the game to your liking. They don't even all have to be dice games. Cards, no matter if just a standard deck or custom cards probably offer even richer possibilities to depict the various events.

Give each player their own face-down stack of cards and create new rules. Require ascending card values, matching suits, high sums, or certain combinations. Allow drawing any number of cards until the right one appears, with the limited card stack representing your energy reserves.

Or, why don't you try a different theme? For example: triathlons, show jumping, or other combined events would offer plenty of fresh material for your new game. What is your favorite sport?

Maybe you also want to experiment with the following "running event": you start with eight dice, can roll them multiple times, and after each roll you must choose a number between One and Six. Only dice with this number can be kept. You must keep at least one die after each roll.

You must choose a unique, not previously used number with each roll. Dice which have been kept once this way cannot be re-rolled anymore.

You decide when to stop rolling and gain as many points as the sum of all kept dice. If you keep rolling until you can keep no more dice, since you already have previously kept dice of the same numbers you've rolled, the entire roll is invalid and you receive no points.

Of course, selecting as many high numbers as possible is important. But when is the right time? Should you settle with your current roll, or start with a lower number because the next one could bring even more points? The situation will become tighter with each new roll.

You can also repeat or stack events to try to reach a certain goal. For example, you can set a goal of 200 or 400 points which can bring even more excitement into the game:

How about a race track with different turns and straights? The roll mechanism decides your progression, though you will have to take the turns with reduced speed and therefore can't choose any high numbers. Advance with each new roll, but don't let yourself veer off the track with an invalid roll, or you have to skip a round.

If you add more risks, you can have them reduce the number of dice more and more, until only a pit stop can help you regain your full power of eight dice. Who will reach the goal first?

CARD HUNT

The last chapter in this book is dedicated to a particular card game which will enthrall novices as well as more experienced players:

Each player starts in the same situation and with the same cards as their opponents. Each player has the same goal—to win as many cards as possible.

All the facts are clearly laid out and the situation is simple. Luck is not a factor. You alone are responsible for your success.

Despite the equal balance of power there is a clear winner each time. And every time, you will have to ask yourself how you can perform better than your opponents.

The more you think about it, the more elusive the events become. Its simplicity makes the game so complicated.

Card Hunt

Number of Players: 2 to 4 (and more)
Length: 10 minutes per single game
Components: 52 cards

Components: a standard deck of 52 cards.

Game idea: All players start with a series of cards from Two through Ace. After playing any card, the players take turns over multiple rounds playing a card with a higher value or passing. Whoever played the last and highest card, receives the whole trick. The goal is to gain as many cards as possible through these tricks.

Setup: At the beginning of the game, sort the cards by suits. Give each player a series of thirteen cards from Two to Ace and agree on who will start the game.

Gameplay: The game consists of individual tricks. Usually, each trick goes over multiple rounds, in which the players will take turns after each other.

The first player starts the trick by playing any card. The second player then has to decide whether to play a higher card or to pass. The game continues like this (even over multiple rounds), with the values of the cards increasing steadily. Whoever has passed once cannot play a card in that trick, even during later rounds.

If it is your turn and the top card played is still yours, meaning that all other opponents have passed, the whole trick is yours. Take the cards and put them face-down in front of yourself.

The next player then starts the new trick with any card of their choice. (Mind this difference compared to most other trick-taking games, in which the player who got the last trick also starts the new one.)

This way, the game continues trick after trick, until one player has played their last hand card. The current trick will then be played until its natural conclusion, after which the game is over.

Scoring: All hand cards that have not been played when the game is over are discarded. These cards are referred to as the fox (the animal who is too smart to let himself be caught). The fox therefore won't be counted for scoring.

The winner is the player who was able to capture the most cards during the course of the game.

Usually, you will play a number of games one after the other. After each game you add the results to a player's total score. At the end, the player with the highest total score wins the game.

Game tactics: At first glance, the game appears to be very simple. However, keep in mind that all players start with the same cards and therefore, the course of the game depends solely on your tactical decisions.

When it is your turn, your most important decision is whether to play a card or if you want to pass. You should consider if the number of cards in the trick is in reasonable proportion to the value of the highest card. (How many cards can you gain there and what is the price?) On the other hand, there is an element of chance involved in winning the trick. (Will all of your opponents pass or can you at least count on being able to still have a turn before an Ace is played?)

To get the trick below, for example, you would have to at least play your king – your second highest card.

Usually, you can expect that no other player will play their Ace for a total of four cards, but you too would pay a rather steep price for three cards. The other player apparently wanted to safely gain two cards using their queen. - The situation in the following example is very different:

Without a doubt, this trick with its six cards is worth some serious consideration and it is still fairly "cheap", as we can gain the upper hand with just a Queen. But what are your chances of actually taking the trick? The next player is unlikely to miss this opportunity to take the cards with a King or an Ace. In the end, your Queen would be for nothing.

Here is the next issue for consideration: if you have decided to play a card, which should you choose? Of course, this depends on the number of cards still left in the game. You should play low enough to keep the price at an acceptable level, but also high enough to make it hard for your opponents to one-up you. In the previous example, this would mean playing the King or even the Ace.

Obviously, deciding when to play your highest cards is of critical importance. Keep track of the highest cards of all opponents to be able to properly evaluate your chances and risks. Your Ace will guarantee you the current trick. If you are the last player to still have your Ace, you can trump any trick and dominate the game this way. Your opponents will always have to fear losing their best cards, whereas you can afford to wait for the biggest trick. In this situation, you should try to make the tricks last long and play as many low cards as possible. This way, the trick will become bigger and bigger or your opponents will have to play high cards, further strengthening your position. Pay attention to when the game is likely to end, though, as to not let your unused chances vanish into nothingness. When asked, players have to reveal the number of hand cards they still have left. You will have to decide on a case-by-case basis whether to force the game to an end or to hold back your hand cards in order to not let your opponents have them.

Variant: Open Card Hunt

As a modification to the regular game, you can also have players play with their cards openly revealed in front of them, instead of having them hidden in their hands.

Theoretically, this changes nothing about the game situation itself, as you also know the cards each player starts with as well as the cards that are played by your opponents.

Still, you will find that the more open information will enable players to deliberate and plan even more, causing the game to have a slightly more strategic character.

Variant: Card Hunt with Passing

As opposed to the regular game, players who have already passed in one round can still play cards during later rounds of the same trick in this variant.

This increases your number of options and tactical decisions when passing. During the course of the game, the number of cards in the hands of each player will now vary even more.

Variant: Fox Hunt

In this variation, the remaining hand cards of the individual players aren't discarded, but count for the player who has ended the game. This puts an entirely new spin on the game. Whoever is able to play all of their cards the fastest will now also get the fox.

Especially when combining Fox Hunt with the previous variant, the decision of playing a card or passing becomes even more important, as the consequences go even further than just the current trick.

Alternatively, you can also try a different way of scoring, using chips (or coins). For that purpose, give each player a certain amount of chips at the beginning. If you have less than thirteen cards at the end of the game, you will pay a chip for each missing card, whereas you will gain a chip for each card you have beyond thirteen. (As all cards are scored, the sum of the chips in the game is unchanged.) This way, you will have a clear overview of the rankings of each player after every single game. At the end, the player with the most chips wins.

Variant: Spot Hunt

Instead of just hunting cards, you could also focus on the actual value of the cards that each player was able to take in their tricks. Each spot card is worth as much as its printed value, whereas face cards and Aces are worth nothing.

This causes a divide between prey (spot cards) and hunters (face cards and Aces). Each player has a total of 54 points in the game. In combination with the other variants you can generate a whole slew of new game ideas.

Variant: Driven Hunt

There is even a compelling variant for more than four players. However, you will also need at least two decks of 52 cards in order to be able to supply all players with their hand cards:

"He that comes last makes all fast" is the motto here, as after each successive game, the player who has the least amount of cards drops out of play. (If multiple players are in the last position with the same amount of cards, they all are out of the game.) This way, the number of players becomes increasingly smaller, until only the last two players will determine the victory among each other.

If you also use the open hands variant, all players who are already out of the game can also follow the game easier and offer their advice as well.

Tactics-wise, you will find yourself in a completely different role, as you usually will only need one big trick to survive. Always keep track of your position compared to that of the other players. Especially focus on the weakest player, and try to starve them out in order to be able to survive yourself.

Alternatively, you can have the player with the least amount of total points after a game knocked out. This way, the individual players will find themselves in entirely different situations, which makes for an exciting asymmetry.

Suggestions

Until now, we were always chasing after the cards. This can be changed, if tricks are now counted negatively and remaining hand cards after the game count against the player. Then, it is all about being able to get rid of their own cards as quickly as possible and avoiding taking tricks – a looking glass world!

SOLUTIONS
TO THE QUESTIONS
IN THE TEXT

Question	from chapter	Solution
1 Three row Complica	Complica	199
2 Trivial Complica	Complica	200
3 Police problem	Excursion into Game Theory	203
4 Silent duel	Excursion into Game Theory	205
5 Probability of total value I	Dice Games from One to Six (Catego)	207
6 Eight rooks	Excursion into Combinatorics	208
7 Poker I	Excursion into Combinatorics	211
8 Coin toss I	Excursion into Combinatorics	214
9 Sensible swaps	Swap	214
10 Average swap values	Swap	216
11 Maximum Unisono	Sono-Games (Unisono)	219
12 Minimum Unisono	Sono-Games (Unisono)	221
13 Probability of total value II	Excursion into Probability Calculation	223
14 Distribution of winnings	Excursion into Probability Calculation	224
15 Coin toss II	Excursion into Probability Calculation	224
16 Poker II	Excursion into Probability Calculation	225
17 Birthday problem	Excursion into Probability Calculation	226
18 Lottery	Excursion into Probability Calculation	227
19 Runs without Sixes	Decathlon	228
20 Shot put	Decathlon	229
21 Pole vault	Decathlon	230

Three row Complica

If Complica is played with only three rows, the first player (White) can win every time, no matter what the second player (Black) does.

After White has started the game in any row, Black has to pick a different one. During their second turn, White should pick the last free row.

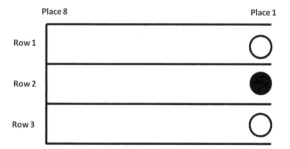

Now, if Black picks the row with their own piece, White will play into the same row and win immediately. Therefore, Black will play into a row with a white Piece. White can then choose the row with the black piece.

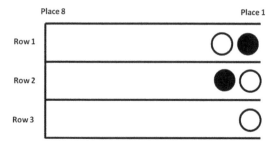

Now, Black will lose no matter what: if they place their piece into the same row as last turn, White will use the same row and win in the first row. However, if Black chooses any other row, White will win in the second row.

Trivial Complica

If you (White) can play into the same row as your opponent (Black) did the turn before, you can ensure a draw with this strategy. (If your opponent places the last piece in a row, you can choose any other row for your next turn.)

As a start, you prevent two black pieces in a row with this strategy. For each black piece that isn't in the first column, you will find a white piece in the next position towards the open end of the row. (Since you have played a white piece in the same row after each black one.) For each black winning line of your opponent, except for the first column, you will find a balancing white line as a result.

Therefore, we conclude that your opponent has to place the first winning line in the first column with his pieces in order to win.

The next step depends on the player order:

If your opponent starts the game, you can always just pick the same row as they do. If it is your opponent's turn, they won't ever find a single black piece in the first column, let alone be able to create a winning line there:

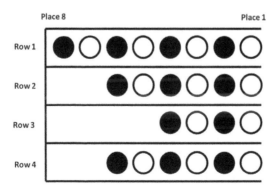

The situation is slightly different when you start the game. Inevitably, you will have to place the first piece into a row. As a result of your strategy, this row will be filled with black and white pieces, with no two of the same color being next to each other in this row, until your opponent will place the last piece, with you unable to react to this as usual. (The row created this way will have white pieces in the second, fourth, sixth and eight columns, so that none of your opponent's winning lines can be created here any longer.)

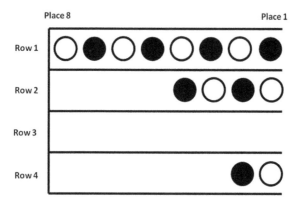

You will have to play into a different row now, sometimes even starting a new one. Only in this situation will your opponent find a black piece in the first column, though all corresponding rows will already be filled.

In order for the first column to have four black pieces, three rows have to be filled completely and the last row must have an even number of pieces. (As you were the starting player, there will always be an even number of pieces on the board after your opponent's turn.)

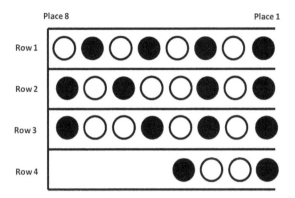

In particular, the deepest piece of this row will be in the second, fourth, sixth, or eighth column, so that no black winning line can be created with it. As there are never two black pieces next to each other within the same row, you will now find a white winning line next to each black one towards the closed end of the board. Consequently, your opponent also won't be able to win the game by having more black winning lines than there are white winning lines.

The strategy described here therefore guarantees a draw. Of course, your opponent also can use the same strategy to ensure a draw – they can't do anything else against your strategy anyway. And for you it then wouldn't make any sense to change your strategy either, as you might only have a worse result as a consequence of your opponent's strategy. A draw therefore represents the best outcome for you as well as your opponent.

....

 Question 3

....

Police problem

You will have the best chances at success if you leave the first two robbers alone and then follow the next robber who could still potentially be the leader – and bigger than the two that came by before. The probability of your success would then be 13/30 or about 43%.

We will call the robbers A, B, C, D and E, depending on their size, with A being the leader. To further clarify, A is the tallest, E is the shortest or, heightwise, A>B>C>D>E.) Apparently, you will now have the following five options to choose from:

Strategy 1: You will become active immediately and follow the first robber who leaves the building.

With this strategy, you will only be successful if the leader is the first person to leave the building. Your probability of success is therefore 1/5 (one in five cases) or 20%.

Strategy 2: You let the first robber go. Afterwards, you will try to become active. The second robber can only be the leader, however, if he is bigger than the first robber. If this is the case, then you follow him. Otherwise, you will wait until another robber who is bigger than the first one and therefore could be the leader leaves the building.

The following table shows all different possibilities. As every possibility is equally likely, we can calculate the average chance of success for Strategy 2 (sum of probabilities divided by number of probabilities).

1st Robber to Leave	Taller Robbers eligible to be followed	Probability that A will be followed	Percentage of A being followed
A	None	0	0
B	A	1	100
C	A, B	1/2	50
D	A, B, C	1/3	33
E	A, B, C, D	1/4	25
Chance of success for strategy 2		5/12	42

For example, the third case in the table tells us that robber C will be the first to leave the building and you will follow – depending on who appears first – either A or B, and that your chance of success is therefore 1/2 or 50%.

Strategy 3: You will let the first two robbers leave. Only then will you try to become active and follow the next potential leader who leaves the building. The following table again shows the possible cases:

1st and 2nd Robbers to Leave	Taller Robbers eligible to be followed	Probability that A will be followed	Percentage of A being followed
A, B	-	0	0
A, C	-	0	0
A, D	-	0	0
A, E	-	0	0
B, C	A	1	100
B, D	A	1	100
B, E	A	1	100
C, D	A, B	1/2	50
C, E	A, B	1/2	50
D, E	A, B, C	1/3	33
Chance of success for strategy 3		13/30	43

Strategy 4: You let the first three robbers leave and only then try to become active.

Strategy 5: You let the first four robbers leave and only try to become active for the last robber.

The probability of the leader being among the first three robbers is 3/5 or 60%. Therefore, the probability of success of strategies 4 and 5 cannot be higher than 2/5 or 40%, so that these strategies are not optimal. Consequently, strategy 3 is the one with the greatest chance of success.

We can actually prove mathematically that the police officer has a roughly 40% chance of success with any number of robbers (as long as that number is known), if he lets about 40% of the robbers leave and then follows the next potential leader.

? Question 4

Silent duel

If you can assume that for each point in time between midnight and 1 am it is equally likely for your opponent to appear, then your best bet is to conduct your raid at exactly 1 o'clock. You will then discover the egg with a probability of 1/2 or 50%, with your opponent having the same chances of having found it earlier.

The outcome of the duel apparently only depends on the order in which the chicken (egg), your opponent, and you become active. The following table gives an overview of all possibilities. (As there are an infinite number of equally likely points in time to choose from, we can disregard the possibility two events happening at exactly the same point in time.) In this table Y = you; O = opponent; E = egg.

Sequence	1st Event	2nd Event	3rd Event	Winner
O-E-Y	opponent	egg	you	you
E-O-Y	egg	opponent	you	opponent
E-Y-O	egg	you	opponent	you
O-Y-E	opponent	you	egg	-
Y-E-O	you	egg	opponent	opponent
Y-O-E	you	opponent	egg	-

For example, the first case (O-E-Y) in the table tells us that your opponent appears first, then the egg appears and you will arrive last and therefore win the egg.

The appearance of the egg and the opponent follows the same random process. (If we switch them, the probabilities stay the same.) Therefore, the sequences O-E-Y and E-O-Y are equally likely. The same is true for E-Y-O and O-Y-E.

With that, the two sequences with which you will be successful (O-E-Y and E-Y-O) are pitted against two equally likely sequences where you won't be successful (E-O-Y and O-Y-E). Consequently, your probability of success cannot be higher than 1/2 or 50%.

If you arrive at exactly 1 o'clock, only the sequences O-E-Y and E-O-Y are possible, which together have a probability of 1 or 100%. As both sequences are equally likely, you optimize your chance of success (O-E-Y) this way with 1/2 or 50%.

Interestingly, this also puts your opponent's probability of success (E-O-Y) at 1/2 or 50%. By telling you their strategy, your opponent can push you into a role in which you both will have equal chances. You will also collectively be in a better position, since one of you is guaranteed to receive the egg.

 Question 5

Probability of Total Value Part I

On average, 2/3 or 67% of all dice rolls will have a total value between five and nine. In contrast, during the course of your eleven rolls during a game you can only expect a value of eleven or twelve once, on average.

Each of the two dice can have one of six different results, so that there are a total of 36 different combinations:

11	21	31	41	51	61
12	22	32	42	52	62
13	23	33	43	53	63
14	24	34	44	54	64
15	25	35	45	55	65
16	26	36	46	56	66

Simply counting the results shows us that 24 of these 36 different outcomes have a total value between five and nine. Therefore, we can expect two out of three rolls to be within that range.

Only three out of the 36 outcomes have a value of eleven or twelve, however, so that we can only expect a result like this only every twelfth roll. With eleven rolls during the course of the game we can therefore expect to roll a high number like this once.

If you want to know more about the occurrence of random events, take a look at our Excursion into Probability Calculation on page 160. There, you will find a thorough examination of the math behind rolling two dice.

 Question 6

Eight rooks

There are 40,320 different possibilities of arranging eight rooks on a chess board so that none are able to capture each other.

As the rooks are able to capture horizontally as well as vertically on the 8 x 8 board, each rook has to be in a different column. If we arrange the eight rooks on the game board with one in each column, each row can also only be chosen once.

The number of possible arrangements therefore also is exactly the different orders of choosing the eight rows of the chess board.

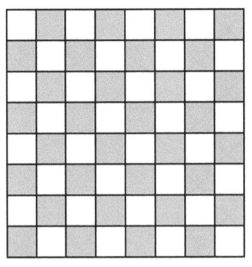

Eight Alternatives

As a result, this ordered selection without duplicates gives us 8! = 8 x 7 x . . . x 2 x 1 = 40,320 different possibilities in total.

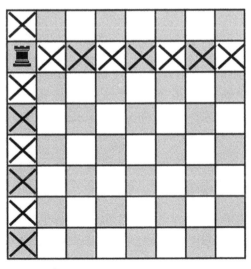

Seven Alternatives

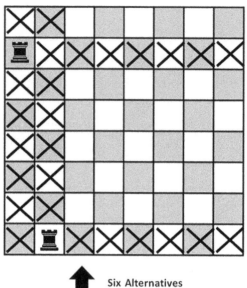

 Six Alternatives

Poker I

1. A player can have a total of 201,376 different card combinations.

   The five dealt cards represent an unordered selection without duplicates from the deck of 32 cards. For this, there are 32 x 31 x 30 x 29 x 28/5! = 201,376 different combinations.

2. A total of 57,344 of these card combinations consist of five different card values. However, 144,032 different card combinations contain at least two of the same value.

   We have eight different card values to choose from. An unordered selection of five different values can be made in 8 x 7 x 6 x 5 x 4/5! = 56 different ways.

After we have determined the five different values, we can choose from four different cards for each of these values. With that, we will have 4 x 4 x 4 x 4 x 4 = 1024 more options to choose from.

With the counting principle, we will have a total of 56 x 1024 = 57,344 card combinations comprised of cards with different values. All other combinations contain at least two of the same value. As a result, there are 201,376 – 57,344 = 144,032 different combinations for this.

3. In all card combinations, three of a kind occurs 12,096 times and there are 224 combinations with four of a kind.

As a start, we will take a look at how often we can expect a combination of three Queens. For this, we will use the same process as with the urn model: from the four available Queens, we can choose exactly three in 4 x 3 x 2/3! = 4 different ways. (Exactly one Queen will be left behind.) For the two other cards in our hand there are 28 x 27/2! = 378 different ways to choose from the 28 other cards in the deck. In total, this gives us 4 x 378 = 1512 different combinations with three Queens, according to the counting principle.

Though, the Queens are only one of eight different card values with which we could have three of a kind. Applying the counting principle again, this gives us a total of 1512 x 8 = 12,096 possible combinations with three of a kind.

Similarly, there are 1 x 28 = 28 different combinations with four Queens, giving us 28 x 8 = 224 different combinations with four of a kind.

4. There are 224 different combinations which only consist of cards with the same suit.

If we only look at the eight Heart cards at the beginning, we can select different cards in 8 x 7 x 6 x 5 x 4/5! = 56 different ways again, while disregarding their order.

With all four suits, the counting principle gives us 56 x 4 = 224 different card combinations which only consist of cards of the same suit.

5. There are 4096 different card combinations with five cards in sequence. 16 only contain cards of the same suit.

As the five cards in sequence are already determined by the value of the lowest card, there are only four different options for the card values contained in such a hand (Seven to Jack, Eight to Queen, Nine to King, Ten to Ace). Each individual value can then be expressed by one of four different cards (different suits). According to the counting principle, this gives us a total of 4 x 4 x 4 x 4 x 4 x 4 = 4096 different combinations.

If the five cards in sequence are also supposed to be of the same suit, we will only have the choice between the four different suits aside from the four different starting values. The counting principle therefore gives us 4 x 4 = 16 combinations.

 Question 8

Coin toss I

Flipping a coin ten times can have 1024 different outcomes. While doing so, there are 252 different possibilities of five heads and five tails occurring

Each individual coin flip can have the result of either heads or tails. The result of the coin flips is therefore an ordered selection of these results and can have a total of 2 x 2 x 2 x 2 x 2 x 2 x 2 x 2 x 2 x 2 = 1024 different outcomes.

We can assume that due to the result of the individual coin flips, the choice between heads and tails is made randomly. The different possibilities of getting heads and tails exactly five times are therefore equivalent with the different possibilities of selecting exactly five of the ten coin flips. This would be an unordered selection without duplicates, with 10 x 9 x 8 x 7 x 6/5! = 252 different outcomes.

Sensible Swaps

When playing Swap, these are the only 20 ways to trade reasonably. (The swaps marked with a double arrow can be traded both ways sensibly and therefore also count twice.)

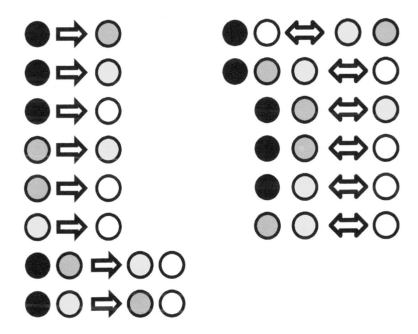

As only one chip per color can be moved during each trade, there are only three different options for each: a chip of that color will be given, received, or not moved at all. If we look at these options individually for each color, we will have 3 x 3 x 3 x 3 = 81 different theoretical options for trades.

In order to consider one of these options as reasonable, we are surely allowed to postulate these three requirements:

1. At least one chip has to be gained.
2. The value of the gained chip cannot be higher than the chip that was given (as per the rules).
3. The colors of the chips gained cannot simply be lower on the order of the colors than the chips given.

By looking at a complete list of all 81 different trading options, you can easily discover that 61 of these theoretical trading options do not fulfill at least one of these conditions. The other 20 swaps result in the group that you see pictured above.

 Question 10

Average swap values

The following diagram shows the average values of the individual colors in Swap:

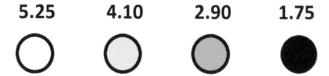

5.25 **4.10** **2.90** **1.75**

The mathematical calculation of these prices is not easy. Therefore, we will solve the problem by complete enumeration (listing and counting all possible cases).

As each individual die can have one of six different results, we will have to consider 6 x 6 x 6 x 6 = 1296 different dice results. As the four numbers are always sorted by their value, many of these results are redundant. (For example, when rolling 6665, it is of no importance whether the 5 was rolled with the first, second, third or fourth die, as it will be assigned to the cheapest color anyway.)

Therefore, we are only interested in all the different possibilities of numbers ordered according to their colors which can occur when rolling the four dice.

The relevant table for this is already known to us from the end of our excursion into combinatorics and will come in handy now. It looks like this:

01x	6666	04x	5555	24x	6431	12x	5542	12x	5322	24x	4321
04x	6665	12x	6554	12x	6422	12x	5541	24x	5321	12x	4311
04x	6664	12x	6553	24x	6421	06x	5533	12x	5311	04x	4222
04x	6663	12x	6552	12x	6411	12x	5532	04x	5222	12x	4221
04x	6662	12x	6551	04x	6333	12x	5531	12x	5221	12x	4211
04x	6661	12x	6544	12x	6332	06x	5522	12x	5211	04x	4111
06x	6655	24x	6543	12x	6331	12x	5521	04x	5111	01x	3333
12x	6654	24x	6542	12x	6322	06x	5511	01x	4444	04x	3332
12x	6653	24x	6541	24x	6321	04x	5444	04x	4443	04x	3331
12x	6652	12x	6533	12x	6311	12x	5443	04x	4442	06x	3322
12x	6651	24x	6532	04x	6222	12x	5442	04x	4441	12x	3321
06x	6644	24x	6531	12x	6221	12x	5441	06x	4433	06x	3311
12x	6643	12x	6522	12x	6211	12x	5433	12x	4432	04x	3222
12x	6642	24x	6521	04x	6111	24x	5432	12x	4431	12x	3221
12x	6641	12x	6511	01x	5555	24x	5431	06x	4422	12x	3211
06x	6633	04x	6444	04x	5554	12x	5422	12x	4421	04x	3111
12x	6632	12x	6443	04x	5553	24x	5421	06x	4411	01x	2222
12x	6631	12x	6442	04x	5552	12x	5411	04x	4333	04x	2221
06x	6622	12x	6441	04x	5551	04x	5333	12x	4332	06x	2211
12x	6621	12x	6433	06x	5544	12x	5332	12x	4331	04x	2111
06x	6611	24x	6432	12x	5543	12x	5331	12x	4322	01x	1111

With this, counting how often the individual prices (dice rolls) occur for the four colors becomes relatively simple. (We will use the same order of White, Light, Dark and Black again. - For example, a five for black only results from the rolls 6665, 6655, 6555 and 5555. This makes for a total of 15 cases out of the 1296 possible ones, so that this price will only occur with a frequency of slightly more than 1%.) The result of counting all possibilities can be summarized thusly:

Price	White	Light	Dark	Black
6	52%	13%	2%	0%
5	28%	28%	9%	1%
4	14%	28%	20%	5%
3	5%	20%	28%	14%
2	1%	9%	28%	28%
1	0%	2%	13%	52%
Average prices	5.25	4.10	2.90	1.75

The average prices can simply be calculated from the individual percentages. (For example, White results in (52 x 6 + 28 x 5 + 14 x 4 + 5 x 3 + 1 x 2 + 0 x 1)/100 = 5.25.)

In order to win, you need an additional chip of each color, meaning a total value of at least 14. Of course, you will try to gain this amount in as few turns as possible. We can use our knowledge of the average prices to analyze the different swaps from the previous question.Each trade changes your stock and consequently your future options. The prices of the future rounds are of course not predictable, but you can base your decisions on the expected average values. Therefore, it also makes sense to assess the possible Swaps based on this.

The expected increase in value during a swap thus results from the difference of the average values of the chips gained and given. (For example, trading a black chip for a white one increases your value by 5.25 – 1.75 = 3.5. This trade is only possible when all four dice show the same number, however, which is very unlikely.)

The detailed calculations show that from the 20 mentioned swaps only 13 actually cause an increase in value. You can find more details about this in the following table:

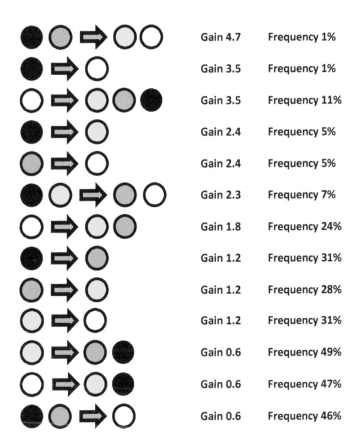

	Gain 4.7	Frequency 1%
	Gain 3.5	Frequency 1%
	Gain 3.5	Frequency 11%
	Gain 2.4	Frequency 5%
	Gain 2.4	Frequency 5%
	Gain 2.3	Frequency 7%
	Gain 1.8	Frequency 24%
	Gain 1.2	Frequency 31%
	Gain 1.2	Frequency 28%
	Gain 1.2	Frequency 31%
	Gain 0.6	Frequency 49%
	Gain 0.6	Frequency 47%
	Gain 0.6	Frequency 46%

....

 Question 11

....

Maximum Unisono

The highest possible score in Unisono is 88 points. Please see the example on the following page.

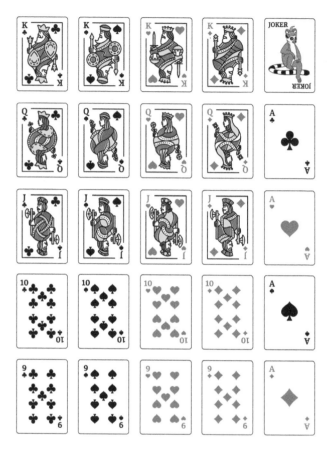

As a start, the example above proves that it is indeed possible to score that many points. Now, we only have to show that it is not possible to gain more than 88 points:

Aside from the Joker, you have four cards for each of the six values. With this, you cannot arrange more than two Quintuplets (the highest scores), four Quadruplets (the second highest scores) and four Straights (the third highest scores). In this respect, the example above is optimal.

However, we still have to concern ourselves with the number of possible Clans. To do this, we will look at Clans consisting of red or black cards and keep in mind that their number together can not be higher than four:

Apparently, there can be a maximum of three Clans per color (with a total of 12 cards of a color and a Joker). If the Clans of a color appear in the rows as well as the columns of the square in the process, there can at most only be one Clan of the other color. (All rows and columns already contain cards of the first color or the Joker.) However, if the Clans of both colors only occur in the rows or the columns, there can only be two Clans of each color due to the number of cards.

Consequently, the total number of Clans in both colors is limited to a total of four. The same is true for Clans consisting of spot and face cards, so that the above example with a total of eight Clans is also ideal in this regard.

 ## Question 12

Minimum Unisono

The lowest possible score in Unisono is 2 points – if the Joker can be used as any card. If the Joker has to be used to result in as many points as possible, the minimum score is 4 points. Please see the example on the following page.

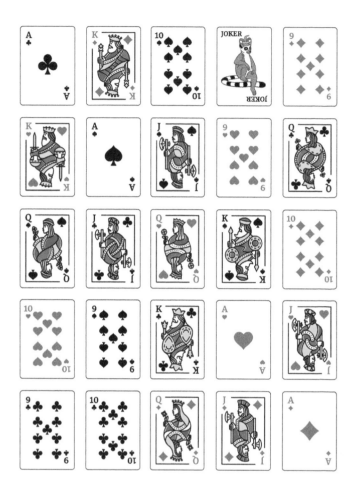

The example above again proves that it is indeed possible to score so few points. Now we also have to make it clear that it is not possible to score even fewer points:

For a line to score no points, it has to contain an Ace as well as a Nine. (Otherwise, it would contain a Pair or a Straight at the very least.) As there are only four Aces and four Nines in the game, there is at least one row and one column left which both score at least one point. Even the Joker can not change this, as it can't be an Ace and a Nine at the same time. Consequently, there is no square with less than two points.

If the Joker has to be chosen to score as many points as possible in the affected lines, there is no way around getting a higher score and you will score at least two additional points.

 Question 13

Probability of Total Value II

When rolling two dice, the sums between two and twelve occur with the following probabilities:

Sum	Probability
2	1/36 = 2.8%
3	2/36 = 5.6%
4	3/36 = 8.3%
5	4/36 = 11.1%
6	5/36 = 13.9%
7	6/36 = 16.6%
8	5/36 = 13.9%
9	4/36 = 11.1%
10	3/36 = 8.3%
11	2/36 = 5.6%
12	1/36 = 2.8%

We base this on the 36 elementary events mentioned in the text and calculate the probabilities by counting the different cases.

? Question 14

Distribution of winnings

When basing our decision on the likelihood of a player winning the game, the wager should be distributed among the two players at a rate of 3:1.

After two more flips at most, the game would have been over. There are four equally likely cases of how the game would have continued: heads-heads, heads-tails, tails-heads and tails-tails.

The first three of these cases would cause the first player to win, whereas only the last case would have led the second player to victory. The chance to win for the first player is 3/4, therefore three times as big as the second player's chance of only 1/4.

? Question 15

Coin toss II

The probability of flipping ten coins resulting in exactly five heads and five tails is 252/1024 or about 24.6%. Having at least six heads will occur with a likelihood of 386/1024, which is 37.7% of all cases.

From our excursion into combinatorics (question 8), we know that the first event happens in 252 out of 1024 cases.

Therefore, there are 1024 − 252 = 772 cases in which there aren't exactly five heads. Apparently, the probability of at least six heads occurring is identical with the probability of having four heads at most (at least six tails). As a result, these 772 cases are equally divided between these two events. This gives us a probability of 386/1024 or 37.7% for having at least six heads.

As exactly one of the three cases we looked at (four heads at most, five heads, at least six heads) has to occur, we will once again have 37.7% + 24.6% + 37.7% = 100% as proof.

 Question 16

Poker II

During Poker with 32 cards, the following is true for the five hand cards:

1. Five different values occur with a probability of 57,344/201,376 or about 28.5%.
2. The probability for having at least two of the same value is 144,032/201,376 or about 71.5%.
3. A three of a kind occurs with a probability of 12,096/201,376 or about 6%, and a four of a kind only in 224/201,376 or about 0.1% of all cases.
4. The probability for a flush is also 224/201,376 or about 0.1%, a straight has a probability of 4096/201,376 or about 2%, whereas a royal flush only occurs in 16/201,376 or about 0.008% of all cases.

We already know these numbers from our excursion into combinatorics (Question 7).

 Question 17

Birthday problem

The probability of at least two people among 23 randomly chosen ones sharing the same birthday is roughly 50.7%.

We disregard leap years and also assume that all 365 days of the year are equally likely as birthdays.

Firstly, we will determine the probability of the birthdays of all 23 people being on different days. For this, we will go through the people individually, one by one:

The first person has their birthday on a particular day. The probability of the second person's birthday being on a different day is 364/365. For the third person, we will now have to exclude two days already, so that their birthday has a probability of 363/365 of being unique amongst them. Similarly, the probability of the birthday being on a different day is decreased with every additional person. For the 23rd and last person, this probability is 343/365.

The probability of all 23 people not sharing the same birthday can now be determined with the multiplication principle, which comes to 365/365 x 364/365 x 363/365 x . . . x 343/365 or about 49.3%. In all other cases, at least two people share the same birthday, so that the probability for this is roughly 50.7%.

Often, people intuitively estimate this to be much lower. This is due to an error in reasoning when we compare a fixed birthday (for example our own) with that of the other 22 people. However, since our excursion into combinatorics, we know that 23 people can form a total of 23 x 22/2 = 253 different pairs, which brings many more opportunities for sharing the same birthday:

 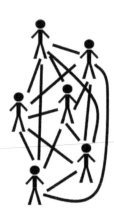

? Question 18

Lottery

The expected value of this lottery is a rounded $9.17. This sum would also have to be the price of the lottery in order to have a fair game.

Rolling two dice is based on the 36 elementary events described in the text. Each number between One and Six occurs in exactly eleven of these elementary events. As a result, the expected value of this lottery is $11/36 \times 30 + 25/36 \times 0 = 330/36 \approx 9.17$. This value does not take into account the $10 price of the lottery.

? Question 19

Runs without Sixes

The following table shows us how many rolls in the individual running events on average will not contain any Sixes:

	100 meters	400 meters	1500 meters
Number of dice used	4	2	1
Percentage of rolls without Sixes	48%	69%	83%
Number of rolls	7	9	13
Average number of rolls without Sixes	3.4	6.3	10.8

In all three cases, the number of the expected rolls without Sixes is considerably higher than the number of relevant rolls in the individual events. If you only take Sixes into account when re-rolling your dice, you will give away some of your potential. Consequently, you should also re-roll some lower rolls which contain no Sixes.

In order to prove the results in the table above, we will refer to what we learned during our excursion into probability calculation:

With one die, we will roll a number between One and Five during five of six rolls or about 83% of all cases. During the 1500 meters we also therefore should not roll a six during 83% of the up to 13 rolls on average, which is about 10.8 rolls.

The probability of only getting numbers between One and Five when rolling two dice is 5/6 x 5/6 = 25/36 or roughly 69%. Only eleven of the 36 possible outcomes contain one or two Sixes. 69% of the up to nine rolls of the 400 meters event will therefore usually not contain any Sixes, which is about 6.3 rolls.

Four dice will roll no Sixes with a likelihood of 5/6 x 5/6 x 5/6 x 5/6 = 625/1296. Therefore, roughly 48% or 3.4 rolls on average should have this quality during the 100 meters.

 Question 20

Shot put

The following table shows the percentage of a shot still being valid after the stated number of throws and how many points on average you will receive for it:

Number of rolls	1	2	3	4	5	6	7	8
Percentage of valid attempts	83%	69%	58%	48%	40%	33%	28%	23%
Average score of valid attempt	3	6	9	12	15	18	21	24

If your attempt already has more than 15 points, you will only lose points on average by continuing.

To prove our results, we will once again use the knowledge gained during our excursion into probability calculation:

With one die, we will roll a number between One and Five in five out of six rolls, or roughly 83% of all cases. The probability of not rolling a six when rolling two dice is $5/6 \times 5/6 = 25/36$ or about 69%. For three dice, the probability is $5/6 \times 5/6 \times 5/6 = 125/215$ or roughly 58%. The other probabilities can be calculated by multiplying the previous result with $5/6$. Ultimately, we have a probability of $5/6 \times 5/6 \times 5/6 \times 5/6 \times 5/6 \times 5/6 \times 5/6 \times 5/6 = 390,625/1,679,616$ or roughly 23% when rolling eight dice.

Each die that doesn't result in a six will bring you an average of three points. The average score of a valid attempt is therefore simply the number of dice times three.

When continuing a valid attempt, we will roll another valid number with a probability of $5/6$, which will bring us an average of three additional points. However, in one of six cases, which is a probability of $1/6$, a Six will appear and cause us to lose all our points for this roll.

If our attempt would currently net us 15 points, the possibility to get an additional three points in five cases is equal to the one case causing us to lose all 15 points. With over 15 points we will only lose points on average.

We can prove this mathematically. From our excursion into probability calculation, we know the expected values of random processes, which is $5/6 \times 3 + 1/6 \times (-15) = 0$ with 15 points and shows us the balance of all the possible outcomes. With more than 15 points, the expected value becomes negative.

Of course, we also have to base our decisions on our previous attempts and not only on the expected value.

Pole vault

During the pole vault, you will have the best chances of successfully jumping the first height of 10 when using four dice. The probability of failing three times in a row here is still roughly 23%, though.

Once again, we will use the knowledge we gained during our excursion into probability calculation and will start by examining jumping with four dice:

In total, there are 6 x 6 x 6 x 6 = 1296 different possible outcomes for rolling the dice. (Each die can show one of six different numbers.) From these, 5 x 5 x 5 x 5 = 625 are rolls that contain no Sixes. (For each die, only the numbers from One to Five are permitted now.)

The following table shows us all possible rolls which contain no Sixes and have a total sum of less than ten:

12x 5211	12x 3321	1x 2222
4x 5111	6x 3311	4x 2221
12x 4311	4x 3222	6x 2211
12x 4221	12x 3221	4x 2111
12x 4211	12x 3211	1x 1111
4x 4111	4x 3111	

Also considering the different combinations to get the rolls listed in the table above, we will have a total of 122 different cases. (For example, the roll 5111 is counted four times, as the Five can occur on four different dice).

As a result, 625 – 122 = 503 of the 1296 possible rolls will enable us to jump the starting height of 10 successfully. The probability for this is 503/1296 or roughly 39%.

Consequently, your jump will fail in 61% of all cases. The likelihood of this happening three times in a row is 61/100 x 61/100 x 61/100 or roughly 23%.

Now, we will also look at your chances when using different amounts of dice:

With two dice, we would have to roll a pair of Fives, which only happens during one of the 36 possible outcomes. With three dice, the following table shows us that in only the listed 53 from a total of 6 x 6 x 6 = 216 cases result in successfully jumping the starting height. The corresponding probabilities are therefore considerably lower than 39%.

1x	555	3x	544	6x	532
3x	554	6x	543	1x	444
3x	553	6x	542	3x	443
3x	552	6x	541	3x	442
3x	551	3x	533	3x	433

When jumping with five (or more) dice, the probability of no Sixes occurring is merely 5/6 x 5/6 x 5/6 x 5/6 x 5/6 = 3125/7776 or roughly 40%. As the sum also has to be at least 10, our chances of success are surely lower than 39% here as well.

CLOSING WORDS

A main problem of our society today is the alleged lack of time. All of us don't have time – time for our families and our friends, time for our nice hobbies and relaxing hours, time for work and, last but not least, time for playing.

Make time for the games in this book. None of them takes longer than half an hour. Allow yourself the leisure of playing and enjoy your time.

In some ways, each society also influences their games. We need a clear concept, short and understandable rules and a manageable playing time. Otherwise it becomes a time sink, which will make the game unplayable for many of us. An interesting mechanism doesn't need to hide behind all kinds of padding. The clearer the goal, the more transparent are our options and the more time we have for the actual game and joy of playing.

Two things are required for every game: the players and the rules. While the people in our gaming groups of course vary, many of us have a totally unnecessary respect for rules, even though we play for entertainment and not just the performance of some sort of predetermined ritual.

We all have different tastes and interests. Therefore, it is only natural to also shape our games individually. Games are dynamic and get their own character in each gaming group. Use the suggestions in this book. Experiment with each game. Develop your own individual, favorite variants. Invent your own game – it is easier than you think!

My thanks go to the publisher Heinrich Hugendubel and his publishing manager Thomas Kniffler for the trustful support of the original German version of this book. I thank Reinhard Schön for his review of the German manuscript and Stefan Wilfert for his dedicated copy-editing of the same.

GAME INDEX

Game	Number of Players	Components	Page
Mr. President	2 or 3	Game board, 52 cards	23
Multego	1 to 4	2 dice, score sheet	81
Obstacle-Jogging	1 to 4	4 dice	109
Open Card Hunt	2 to 4	52 cards	191
Open Sono	2	52 cards, 1 Joker	147
Open Unisono	1	52 cards, 1 Joker	152
Parliament	3 to 5	2 x 52 cards	98
Quasono	4	52 cards, 1 Joker	153
Relay-Jogging	1 to 4	4 dice	109
Sellout	1 to 4	4 dice, 4 x 12 chips	129
Seventeen	2 to 4	6 dice, score sheet	75
Six Hundred	1 to 4	6 dice, score sheet	66
Sono	2	52 cards, 1 Joker	142
Spot Hunt	2 to 4	52 cards	192
Strategic Sono	2	52 cards, 1 Joker	147
Subito	2 to 4	2 x 52 cards	135
Swap	1 to 4	4 dice, 4 x 12 chips	123
Sway Swap	1 to 4	4 dice, 4 x 12 chips	128
Thirty-six	2 to 4	6 dice, score sheet	74
Tower of Babel	2 or 3	52 cards, 3 Jokers, 1 die	19
Unisono	1	52 cards, 1 Joker	151
Versatility-Jogging	1 to 4	4 dice	108
Vox Populi	3 or 4	Game board, 2 x 52 cards	27

CPSIA information can be obtained
at www.ICGtesting.com
Printed in the USA
BVHW062328091122
651574BV00005B/118